The Career Equation®

The Career Equation®

Coaching a Culture of Career Conversations

Erica Sosna

 Open University Press

Open University Press
McGraw Hill
8th Floor, 338 Euston Road
London
England
NW1 3BH

email: enquiries@openup.co.uk
world wide web: www.openup.co.uk

First edition published 2021

A catalogue record of this book is available from the British Library

ISBN-13: 9780335249053
ISBN-10: 0335249051
eISBN: 9780335249060

Library of Congress Cataloging-in-Publication Data
CIP data applied for

Typeset by Transforma Pvt. Ltd., Chennai, India

Printed in Great Britain by Bell and Bain Ltd, Glasgow

Praise page

The Career Equation is must-read text for parents, personal tutors, HR managers, team leaders, careers advisers and coaches. An easy guide for importance career conversations in our ever-changing environment. It's never too soon to start a career conversation. Erica reaffirms that we operate within a disrupted job market and may need to reinvent ourselves multiple times during our working lives. The text takes us step by step through the elements that need to be considered. The Career Equation dispels some of the myths of career advice and offers a solid solution for career choice for the twenty first century."

Dr Helen Smith, Faculty Head of Coaching and Mentoring for
Business and Law, Department of People and Performance

This book is a great resource for career professionals, offering tools and ideas that get to the heart of what we mean by career success. Navigating a career positively means finding a healthy balance between what you want to get out work and what work takes out of you. The Career Equation concept here offers great framework for coaches and managers to help others work out much more fruitful career deal.

John Lees, Author of How to Get A Job You Love

I found The Career Equation to be very informative and pertinent. It focuses on what is important - thriving in our working environment and in our careers, that I believe influences our quality of life. This book helps to discover the simple and effective model that has enabled me to have valuable career conversations, and more importantly, see the positive results when individuals are making the choices aligned to their strengths and passions. If we would all thrive in our careers, how amazing would that be!?

Aneta Jajkowksa, People & Organisation Partner /
Your Career Plan Accredited Coach

For my mother Claire and my father Boris, who came to the UK from India and Russia and made a life for themselves from scratch. You taught me the value of doing work you love, learning new things and applying yourself to be the very best you can be at whatever you put your mind to. Thank you for this education in life.

Contents

1 And so we begin …

What do you want to be when you grow up?

We love asking our kids this question. Yet really, how do we expect them to know the answer? In truth, lots of us are still trying to answer this question for ourselves, as big old adults! An estimated 70 per cent[1] are thinking about or are on the hunt for a new job, and 85 per cent[2] actively dislike the work they do. So, Houston, we definitely have a problem.

I first noticed that this was the case in 2000. I was a bit of a swot, so when I graduated, I returned to my school to let my headmistress know that I had accepted a job in the Civil Service Fast Stream graduate scheme. While she was pleased for me, she had a slightly perplexed look. When I asked her why, she shared that she thought I 'might have done something more creative'. I was gutted. If she had seen that creativity in me early on and thought that there was work that would suit my character, why had she not told me in the seven years I had spent at the school? Were there other choices that I could have made?

I had taken what I thought was the 'right and sensible' route and this is where I had ended up. Somewhere I had picked up that I could not allow work to be fun and adventurous and suit my character. I needed to do 'serious' work and have a 'proper' job, and so I made my way into government. Yet the truth was that as I left her office, I already had an inkling that even though my new role was impressive, it might not be the right fit for me.

As a social historian, I've always been very interested in why we all do what we do and how this is influenced by the beliefs, norms and needs of society, family and economy. It strikes me that there is no greater risk or opportunity than how we spend our time. Our lifetime. Psychology tells us that we want this time to matter and have meaning. We want to feel good about what we do. And successful at it. Yet we all define success in very different ways, so how do we measure these obscure ideas of success, fulfilment and meaning?

I began this work because I wanted an answer to this big question – for myself, as an individual who had struggled to make a good decision about her

---

1   https://www.mhanational.org/sites/default/files/Mind%20the%20Workplace%20-%20 MHA%20Workplace%20Health%20Survey%202017%20FINAL.PDF

2   https://news.gallup.com/opinion/gallup/171632/gallup-releases-new-insights-state-global-workplace.aspx

career path – more of my story later – for others, so that they might thrash about for less time than I did, and lastly, for the client organizations that my company serves so that, in helping their people find direction and make good choices, they could compete for and keep the very best talent.

For the most part, this book is about using a practical model to bridge the careers gap. Somewhere between formal education and careers advice, there arose a gulf. Young people struggled to acquire the self-knowledge about who they were and what they were good at and apply this to the world of work. Even older people, who had more understanding of who they were and a wider base of experience of the world of work, often doubted whether they were in the right role, or compromised what they wanted in order to 'make do' and have a job of some kind. Too often, people fell into careers that were mismatched with their unique, personal design. This can occur because of peer pressure or expectation from our families to follow in the footsteps – 'All us Smiths are doctors'. Or perhaps there is an expectation to do better than the previous generation and 'professionalise'. Or even a lack of awareness of the roles that are out there that are a good fit with our character and interests.

There's an underlying question here: whose job is it to help you find your right career? Is it your parents'? Teachers'? Manager's or coach's? The reality is that this work is often a little about retrofitting. We're working with adults to address a gap that should be a continuous dialogue from childhood. And because we are working with organizations, we need to work within the structure – making internal coaches, external coaches that are subcontracted in and the manager population the go-to audience for this work. Whoever is tasked with the job, there is real value in a method to realign a person's core skills and talents with the right role in the business, or even outside of it.

Misalignment between someone's key gifts and the job at hand might, at best, mean they were distracted from giving their all to the job and, at worst, result in burnout, depression, frustration and truly dire performance. In short, a lose/lose for everyone.

Thus, over my working life, I've taken my investigations into what makes for a fulfilling career choice and made this my specialism, so that I might help other humans solve this problem.

This book offers a solution.

In my many years as a career coach, I began to notice that there were a huge number of worries, concerns and criteria impacting career decision making. It was almost as if people were overwhelmed by choices. This, combined with their emotional reaction to change, or burnout, or a career mismatch, made the conversation loaded and complex. I wanted to create a simple model to streamline this conversation and bring clarity to the issues at hand – a model that would work for any industry, stage of life, working pattern or level of seniority. To accomplish this, I started to focus on what the key 'buckets' of decision-making variables were. The patterns that I noticed were distilled into what is now known as the Career Equation®.

Figure 1.1 Too many choices lead to paralysis

Too many choices lead to paralysis

Illustration by Bojan Spasic, bojanspasic.com

Why this book matters to you

The thing is, we spend an awful lot of time at work. Up to 80,000 hours in fact.[3] And yet, at least here in the UK, we have very little in the form of a definitive approach to helping young people and adults find or rediscover their ideal career direction. Most of us fell into our careers rather than chose them. Too many choices can lead to paralysis. This rather haphazard approach to deciding how to spend these 80,000 hours tends to continue into adulthood. And even those adults

---

3 https://www.independent.co.uk/life-style/british-people-work-days-lifetime-overtime-quit-job-survey-study-a8556146.html

who began with a career that excited them and suited them, may still find themselves at choice points in their lives where they want to step into something new and yet have no methodology to be able to confidently assess their options.

This is the gap I've made it my business to solve.

Who is this book for?

This book is addressed to anyone working in an advisory role concerning the careers of others and who wants to improve their toolkit to do so. I've written it mostly with those working in an organization in mind: for those of you who are in-house talent, learning or performance professionals. Yet it will also be valuable to teachers, careers advisers, independent coaches and mentors who want to help their clients make the most of their careers and achieve maximum personal satisfaction from their work.

Thought experiment

Are you off on holiday this year? What kind of research have you done to prepare? How many conversations have there been about what you and your holiday partners want out of the break? Have you compared costs and shopped around for a deal? Perhaps you identified a shortlist of locations or places to stay based on a set of criteria that matter to you, if you are going solo, or to you and your travel companions. Now consider the amount of time you have put into planning your career. I'm willing to bet it's less time than you have spent on your two-week break in the South of France.

Interesting, right?

I called my company Career Matters because, well, it does! Career and the work we do is inextricably linked with our sense of self. A fulfilling career can give us fantastic learning, a great network, super opportunities to travel or try new things, financial stability and a strong identity. Conversely, the wrong role can cost us emotionally and physically, lead to burnout, lost productivity and poor health, and crush our self-esteem. Yet careers are loaded – we may be under pressure to fulfil our parents' hopes and dreams, or just overwhelmed by choice or under pressure to bring in the money, regardless of our fit, by going with the first role that is offered.

The current context

The twenty-first century is the time of the fourth industrial revolution. This revolution is transforming the way we work, where we work, when we work and whether we work at all! The first part of this book will set out the challenges of this evolving environment in more detail, but let's take a quick look at the headlines.

When individuals come to our programmes or 121 consultations, they present the following kinds of problems. See how many ring a bell for your talent.

- I sort of landed in this role and don't really know what suits me.
- I've outgrown this role but don't know who to talk to.
- The job sort of fits me but I wonder if I might prefer to do something completely different.
- I love this work. Is there room for me to grow and what is the next step?
- How do I choose the right role for me?
- If I don't want my boss's job, what else could I do?
- I've lost my career mojo but not sure why.
- I'm worried I have left it too late to do what I really love.
- My profession is undergoing major upheaval and I'm not sure I want to stay in it.
- I have so much more to give but have no idea who to talk to about it or how to say it.
- My job is no longer relevant/needed/in existence.
- I've been pigeonholed and want to show others I have more to offer.

These seem like a diverse range of problems and questions. Yet the answer to all of them comes down to one simple thing. To make a confident choice about their next steps, the questioner needs to be able to articulate what matters most to them when it comes to their job.

We spend very little time explicitly exploring this. Yet we all want to talk to someone about our careers. And if your talent are not talking to you, then they are likely talking to head-hunters and the competition.

Career conversations

'But hang on ... if we talk to them about their careers, won't we just be coaching them to leave?'

This is probably the most common objection we hear when introducing career conversations and the Career Equation® to a new client organization. I get it. It seems counter-intuitive to explore a person's next career move while they are comfortably delivering well in a role they may only recently have acquired. Why open Pandora's box and risk that you might talk them out of the company? Ok, it could lead to finding them new opportunities in the business, but what if that move takes them outside the firm?

Yet here is the thing. People want to talk about their careers. They want a sounding board. They need to have a sense of where their skills and interests could take them and make informed decisions about their next steps. So, they will seek out someone to talk to.

Surely, it's better that the person they have that conversation with is you. If the appropriate talent managers are privy to their needs and concerns, you are more likely to be able to help them see that their future is with you. Might their horizons stretch further than your firm? Of course. Yet again, when we consider it rationally, isn't it better to know this in advance, to have been able to make handover plans and to have exhausted all the internal options together than to receive a surprise, last-minute resignation and then have to scramble to replace them?

Other worries that make managers and coaches reluctant to talk careers with their talent include being short of time, being afraid that they will have to say yes to any request made or not feeling confident they have the skills and the structure to have the right kind of conversation at the right time. This book will address all of these concerns and provide you with practical actions and agendas on which to hang a high-quality conversation.

What's in it for my firm?

Most of our client organizations have some major pain points around careers. I'll be taking you to meet a number of key individuals and share how we used the Career Equation® to troubleshoot in their firms, so let's drop in and hear some of their concerns.

Companies present with the following issues:

> Everyone knows our grad scheme is the best in class. It wins awards year after year. So, the competition wait till our graduates qualify and then they circle in and try to poach them. We'd like to get better at career conversations with this population so that they have a plan for a future with us and aren't tempted by an offer from one of our competitors that may be enticing in the short term but would actually take them away from the best brand in the business.
>
> Director and Head of Learning and
> Development, international property company

> We need our high potentials to feel in charge of their own destiny and be able to forge their own path. They need to own their careers and plan their next moves to get to senior leadership. Having a plan for their next strategic moves gives them a continued incentive to grow with us.
>
> Krissie Haigh, global talent expert and
> business psychologist

> We need our talent to specialise early. As we have grown through acquisition, they often feel like they haven't really got their heads round the brands and opportunities before they make this decision. Result? They leave to join another firm where the choices may be more narrowly defined. They are

simply overwhelmed by choice. We need to act as career coaches, helping them to define what they want and then as recruiters, finding the roles in the company that are a good match with what interests and motivates them.

HR POP and Grad Scheme Designer,
Dassault Systèmes

We definitely want our managers to be discussing careers and future opportunities in our company. Yet they don't always feel comfortable to initiate the conversation.

Director of Talent Development, international
technology company

It's too easy for us as a leadership team to make assumptions about what our talent want. We end up being more of a hindrance than a help by taking development decisions without direct input from them. This can also lead to claims of favouritism. We want to make decisions about who to offer our special projects to, based on their interests and desires. But how do we find these out?

Chief Financial Officer, financial company

People are very proud to work here and in the social mission more generally. As a consequence, people tend to have longer than average tenure and turnover is historically low. But growth and mobility – sideways and upwards – within the university has been limited at times by siloed and hierarchical constraints.

Our ambition – in parallel to streamlining our talent and resourcing practices – was to instil new confidence in our people, liberating them from some of their own limiting beliefs and building skills to help them take charge of their career. Ultimately, it's our belief that the only way we create the dynamic and inclusive culture required to support our students transform their own lives, is to make sure that our staff are empowered to realise their own potential.

Head of Talent and Development,
The Open University

For real results, both the employer and employee, or coach and coachee, need to be having a discussion using the same model. We need to be sure that we are talking about the same things and understand one another fully.

If we don't unearth some of the assumptions we are making around careers, we can make mistakes. I believe that I have found a way to eliminate this, without us falling into some of the common pitfalls that make managers fearful of these kinds of conversations (more on this later).

In this book, I will provide you with a new understanding of what a career is, how we measure satisfaction in your career and how a simple word equation can be deployed to achieve a wide range of positive results.

I will give you the context on how and why this matters, and offer the business case both for the individual and for the organization to get good at having insightful, personalised career conversations. I will break down and share our potent process for career navigation, and together we will analyse how this model can be used to identify the core gifts and capabilities of your talent.

Through this process you will gain important insight into the drivers that really matter to your people and will be able to guide them to use this insight in a simple way to identify the right opportunities and career paths for them.

When you do this, you will not only enable them to do remarkable things. Both you and your organization will be recognised as exemplary developers of people, able to unlock performance, satisfaction and retention.

Used well, a career conversation can become a true lever for an intimate understanding of the person in front of you. It can transform the quality of your relationship. It can help them achieve real clarity about what they want out of their career and identify where they can do their best work. For organizations, this leads to phenomenal retention and engagement. For independent coaching professionals, it leads to a string of referrals and lots of fantastic case studies. Excited? Me too! Let's dive in. Let's start with the big picture as it stands in 2021?

2 Why this matters now

The big influences

When I was a social history student, I once took a course on the history of manners. It's an extremely interesting field because manners demonstrate the changing shape of attitudes, beliefs, behaviours and how we relate to each other. Manners were the way in which the elite determined who was 'in' and who was 'out'. They were a way to spot 'people like you', so the rules would change regularly in order to catch people out. Heaven forbid that the hoi polloi caught up with the latest manners and bluffed their way into the upper classes!

Manners are easy to research because there were books written on them and they were updated regularly. These Debretts style books were about what to do and not to do in polite company. Over time, the unusual, new rules became a norm that more and more people, at most levels of society, took for granted. In this way, novel ideas and expectations filtered through to become a common and mainstream expectation.

Take, for example, the history of the handkerchief and the 'right' way to sneeze. Today, we accept without question that it is only polite and hygienic to avoid sneezing in the direction of others and that it is important to capture the unintended debris in a paper or fabric handkerchief. But this was not always so. Early manners books needed to instruct those at the dinner table not to sneeze directly onto someone else's' food, but there is no mention of using fabric to contain the snot. Some years later, in the *Manual of Politeness* (1860), we are told to face away from the table and put our handkerchief away. The use of handkerchiefs is also not limited to the blowing of noses. The Victorians even created an elaborate secret language of flirting using nothing more than a lacy kerchief. Now, perhaps, the fabric sneeze cloth seems a little old-fashioned and we tend to use a disposable tissue, or at the very least our hands or elbows.

What this little aside demonstrates is that our views and perspectives about what is acceptable to do, think and say are changing all the time. Changes in technology (the ability to buy fancier cloth), access to global markets and the ability to travel and trade with them (affording us a broader range of perspectives and people), and changes in mores and fashion (led by thought-leaders, innovators and marketeers) all have an enormous impact on our perspectives about what is desirable or possible for us to think, buy or do. Leaps of perspective make something that was once acceptable and commonplace, unacceptable or in need of a radical rethink.

It is through these leaps that the abolition of slavery, the introduction of universal free healthcare in the UK or the right of women to own property, came about.

These kinds of leaps are also to be found in perspectives and aspirations around work. Let's take a deeper look at how technology, global mobility and changing aspiration impact employment and our expectations of our careers.

The impact of technology

You may have heard that we are currently undergoing the fourth industrial revolution, also known as the Digital Revolution. Industrial revolutions are points in time where a leap in the evolution of processes for manufacturing and transporting goods and services takes place.

The industrial revolutions and their leaps

Leap 1: The Industrial Revolution (1780–1840) – we move from handmade to manufactured production of goods.

Leap 2: The Technical Revolution (1870–1920) – we benefit from technological advances such as electricity and communication networks such as the telephone and the railways.

Leap 3: The Scientific-Technical Revolution (1940–1970) – mainstream computer technology evolves, and biotech is born.

Leap 4: The Digital Revolution (1995 onwards …) – advances in cloud computing, the internet and digitization of information and communication enable connectedness and speed over a vast distance.

The danger of the 'great leap forward'

In every leap we have taken as humanity, there was a risk. That risk was that the existing skills would no longer be as valuable and that certain jobs would no longer be needed as the new machines took over. In each instance, we were right to be worried.

The Luddite uprising in 1811[1] was a protest by unskilled weaving and textile workers, who began smashing up weaving machinery, because they rightly recognised that it would mean less work for some of the poorest and least skilled workers in society.

Similar fears are justifiably voiced when it comes to the Digital Revolution.

We know the robots are coming. They're taking our jobs. They are already making their presence felt in a number of fields, proving themselves more

---

1 https://www.historic-uk.com/HistoryUK/HistoryofBritain/The-Luddites/

accurate and faster than humans. Bots are to be found providing answers to simple customer service queries, revising legal contracts and sifting job applications for the right keywords. While the speed at which machines can learn can far outstrip human capacity to share knowledge, their use also comes with risks not just to job security, but to system malfunction.

Robot doctors are now making diagnoses of disease.[2] What if these doctors, worldwide, could receive an update on the latest effective cancer treatment? Within moments they would all be up to date with the very cutting edge of healing. Compare this to the journals, conferences and knowledge sharing of the human population. However, consider what would happen if the wrong update got sent, or the system was hacked – much more potential damage to human life could occur, at much greater speed.

Key: We need to be able to compete with the artificial intelligences, finding unique niches that they cannot attend to, or at least be able to work effectively alongside them in what Deloitte called 'Superjobs', partnerships between human and robotkind. This presents an interesting challenge for management and leadership, as robots aren't paid and are immune to performance management or motivation by values and recognition. It will be fascinating to see how these partnered workplaces evolve over time.

In every crisis there is an opportunity

Again, in every historic technological leap, as jobs were lost, so new jobs were also created. With the Scientific-Technical Revolution really kicking off around the 1950s and ramping up into the new millennium, the number of new roles exploded. In the last decade, a whole set of skills, job roles and job titles were created that just had not existed before. The fields of engineering, the internet, online shopping and 3D design have transformed the skill sets required in these industries and created a whole new set of requirements, including skills in social media, virtual worlds and coding. This brand new set of skills and roles triggered a real disconnect between the existing education system and the world of work – as the previous system was designed to create a long tenured quiet, compliant employee, with the skills to memorise and execute tasks. Suddenly a new set of skills and level of technological literacy were going to be needed, and education struggled to keep up.

In the Digital Revolution, we have seen an enormous proliferation of new roles in 3D design, search engine optimization, website building, coding,

---

2   https://www.bbc.co.uk/news/technology-44635134

machine learning, product development and many more. These role titles are less familiar to us; they have necessitated a new language. The activity involved in the role is more ambiguous and a lot less easy to immediately understand. Whereas most of us would be able to bring to mind what a doctor, teacher or miner might do all day, 'senior product engagement managers' may be harder to see clearly in our mind's eye. This has made good careers advice harder to give as the range of jobs cannot be held by one mind alone.

An interesting outcome of this proliferation is that it creates more opportunity to try something new. Whereas professions rather tie us to them, moving from one form of law to another or one school to another provides varied workplaces in the same vein. Roles such as search engine optimization or project management provide more opportunity to move across a range of industries without needing to retrain or start again.

It's my view that this explosion of new roles is likely to continue – perhaps even to the point of making a job title and a formal progression path impossible to name or map. In these times, it will be important to define your value by the skills you bring and the way you use them to add value, rather than a track record in a specific profession per se.

Key: Successful workers in the future will be agile in their movement across industries, roles and activities, and able to articulate their skills and value. To do so, they need to be able to distil their key attributes and have the self-knowledge to correctly identify where they can be most useful.

New roles, new education

To make the most of these opportunities for mobility, we may need to be able to quickly retrain or acquire new skills. This has become easier than ever. Again, whereas the previous world view was that education was a long-term investment, it has now been possible to take shorter courses, some at a distance, to qualify in key desirable skills such as agile project management or design thinking.

The large universities have begun to feel the impact of this, as many students choose free MOOCs (massive online open courses) or short digital courses run by niche specialists rather than returning to take an MA or undertake teacher training. This is not to say that people will not continue to invest in a three-year higher education programme, but rather that education that is keeping pace with the modern-day workplace is more likely to be provided by leaner outfits that can offer just-in-time solutions and qualifications in a shorter period of time. These may also be delivered in a more practical and less academic format and cost less than the recently inflated university fees (thus arguably offering better value, or at least a different kind of value).

In the digital age, the technologies that will be needed for success will be changing across every industry. Adapting to these changes and learning new things, through post-formal education methods, will be crucial, whether you are a farmer, in government, the arts, banking or manufacturing. These new technological skills, including design thinking, project management and innovation as well as hard skills in coding and design and online presence building, will be more transferable. This will lead to greater mobility across industries and more options for seasoned professionals with specialist, valuable skills to move seamlessly across companies in different sectors or to move quickly into new roles in the same company in response to changes in market or consumer demand.

Key: The opportunity to retrain has become much more affordable and achievable, with niche providers offering specialist technical education in a just-in-time model. This allows for much better adaptability and flexibility in career management.

The job for life is dead

It was not so long ago, perhaps just beyond my parents' generation, that the job for life was an expectation. People landed in their roles and in their organization and were expected to stay in them until retirement. A change in the industrial set-up in your local area could have an enormous impact on your job opportunities and sense of identity. We only have to look at the impact of the closure of the coal mines to see that this was true.

However, the question of whether you actually liked your work, and whether it was in line with your skills and what you enjoyed, was rarely a consideration. Social mobility was also a lot more restricted and prescriptive than it is today – though there is undoubtedly still work to be done.

In addition, back then there weren't that many job families and access to these roles was restricted by both class and education. As a result, careers advice was pretty simple. If you were working class, your options were typically manual labour, the trades and agriculture or transport. If middle class and literate, perhaps a role in an office or in healthcare. Only the upper classes, even as late as the 1970s, could access higher education and thus consider a career in law, the civil service or technology. And of course, gender still played an enormous role in choices, where women were expected to take up jobs such as secretary, nurse or waitress. Once you had been allocated your role in life – either because you went into the family trade or profession, or you took what was available to keep your head above water – well, there you were likely to stay.

This expectation extended to employers too. They could reasonably expect that their staff were not likely to defect to another company or to commence a completely different profession with a great deal of frequency. An administrative clerk in an accounting firm was unlikely to do a bunk to retrain as a carpenter and thus 'find himself'.

Nowadays, the average time in a job has come down to just four years. Few professionals will stay in the same job, or even the same industry, for a very long stretch any more. As a result, today's school-leavers can be expected to have up to 12 jobs over their working life.[3] Greater mobility has meant even more choices. Yet the luxury of choice can itself be debilitating. Too many options can be overwhelming. In the last five years, we have seen an enormous reduction in average duration in a role. I remember when my tenure of two years in each of my jobs was looked on with concern – it would not now result in even a mildly raised eyebrow. Instead, we are asking are we ok to stay in a job we enjoy for longer than the average shelf life? What does this rapid turnover mean for job security (for the employee) and for business continuity (for the employer)? Do we even want to be employed at all if we could be reasonably sure of regular work on a project or freelance basis? These choices can result in a culture of jumping ship as soon as an alternative makes itself available – the 'grass is always greener' effect.

Key: Those who are able to make the most of this disrupted job market will be those who know what they are looking for and what it is that they offer. We will need to be able to define the key criteria for our own unique career decisions and block out the clamour of alternative voices and perspectives. It will be important to be able to own your career story, explaining how you get to certain decisions about role, education and career pivots.

Changing aspirations

At some point between the time I graduated in 2000 and the current day, there was a shift. Like the manners books of old, what expectations of work mean for people began to change. For many people, the question of whether they liked what they did and how well it suited their skill set began to be of real importance. In addition, as corporate social responsibility began to surface, we began to be bothered by the ethics and values driving the companies we worked for. As we gained rights around working hours and the EU working time directive was introduced in 2003, we started to expect that our employers would be interested in our well-being. And the growth of psychometrics and personality profiling meant both employers and employees started to want to match skills to personality. Recruiters and occupational psychologists discovered that productivity and performance could be impacted by matching the person to the role, and that a bad fit could massively affect our well-being.

These trends all began to shift our expectation of what work could give us. Now we wanted work that had meaning and purpose, it became more important to us to have a big 'why' for our careers, beyond financial security. Relative economic prosperity in the Western world over the 2010s had generated the luxury of self-actualization and personal development, having the 'right' to decide how you want to spend your 80,000 hours. This new thinking has meant that the unacceptable is no longer acceptable.

---

3 https://www.thebalancecareers.com/how-often-do-people-change-jobs-2060467

Never has this been more visible in the young. The 'Millennials' and derogatory terms such as 'snowflakes', used to ridicule young adults, has indicated a dislike for what is perceived to be an overly sensitive generation of employees. Yet this generation is not shy in sharing their expectation that work should be valuable and even fun, and they are unafraid to express their dismay when values and boundaries are breached. Perhaps they have much to teach about what should and should not be endured in the workplace.

Whereas the most desired job for a graduate in 2000 might have been in investment banking, these days the aspiration is to run a start-up from the beach in Porto or Bali. One of the top graduate employers in the UK is Teach First,[4] an aspirational charity that diverts high-achieving students and mature career changers into teaching rather than a more traditional professional choice. Their popularity and appeal are in no small part due to wanting to be part of something meaningful, part of a community making a difference, and their strong brand as change agents for the future. Employer brand experts ignore this at their peril.

It's not just the young or the carefree either. Parents too are changing their view. Men are leaving jobs in order to spend more time parenting. In fact, a recent research report from the University of London indicated that fathers are spending 700 per cent more time with their children[5] than my father did with me in the late 1970s and early 1980s. This time has to be taken from somewhere, and more and more fathers are choosing to sacrifice workplace time in favour of time with their families.

We're also seeing a shift towards more stay at home parenting roles being fulfilled by fathers. So, across the board, quality of life is becoming as much, if not more, of a priority as the work itself. Work has to work on our terms.

Key: We want our 80,000 hours to count for something. We are beginning to ask existential questions about the place and function of work in our lives. Many of us would like to see more of a purpose to our employment than simply putting food on the table.

The digital nomad

Alongside the desire to work on something that matters is the desire to work in a way that suits the modern lifestyle. Technology combined with cheap travel has exploded the job market in a fascinating way.

Whereas we may previously have been limited by geography and commutable distance with our job choices, many service and knowledge roles can now

---

4   https://www.standard.co.uk/futurelondon/skills/uk-graduate-schemes-2019-london-employers-best-grad-jobs-a4138311.html

5   https://www.theguardian.com/lifeandstyle/2014/jun/15/fathers-spend-more-time-with-children-than-in-1970s

be carried out from anywhere in the world. This means talented professionals can be recruited and employed from across the globe, as part of a virtual team. Employees can work for firms headquartered elsewhere and with limited real-world contact with their team members in other parts of the world. This global talent pool is a huge opportunity for employers stretching the net wide for the best talent. It is also an opportunity for the professional seeking either to travel and work, as a digital nomad, or to find work that they enjoy without being constrained by the local market or disrupted by the upheaval of relocation.

Of course, this is not true for every role. There are plenty of jobs that still require a real-world presence – such as surgeons, waste disposal teams, waiters and musicians … but our experience of lockdown in 2020 and the technological experiences we had access to may lead to even these jobs having a work from home option! Imagine being served by a virtual waiter or experiencing remotely controlled surgery? Maybe and maybe not …

Key: Global talent pools mean access to opportunities and talent is greater than ever before. Career changers in some professions are no longer restricted by needing to be local to the role. Technology will continue to accelerate and disrupt the way work is done.

The gig economy and freelancing/micropreneurs

Fiverr, Top Talent and Upwork. Three platforms that have fundamentally disrupted the way we spend time and earn money. All three take out the middleman and bring the service provider in direct contact with the buyer. This rise in the gig economy (and the sharing economy, with platforms such as Airbnb or Camplify) has led to a new range of freelance roles, where work can be performed around other commitments or alongside a formal job in the form of a 'side hustle'.

For some, the gig economy has liberated them from the shackles of employment. For others it is a necessary evil to keep food on the table. Whatever the perspectives, it is clear this project-based economic activity is here to stay.

A 2016 report from McKinsey investigated the level of choice influencing those in the gig economy. It was clear that there is a substantial gap between those who take on short gigs out of financial necessity versus those who choose to add a side project or are sure that they wish to pursue an independent, freelance career.

Roughly those figures break down as:

- 30 per cent are free agents who actively seek freelance opportunities as a career lifestyle
- 40 per cent have a casual side project that supplements their income
- 14 per cent would rather not work in the gig economy but reluctantly choose to do so, and

- the remaining 16 per cent consider it a way to supplement an income that would otherwise be insufficient to meet their basic necessities.[6]

The Office for National Statistics reports that the number of freelancers in the UK has grown from 3.3 million to 4.8 million in the last two decades.[7] An autonomous way of working is becoming an increasingly popular choice.

Companies are also becoming more fluid in their head-count. Many are downsizing and outsourcing in order to have more flexibility in their operations. There are increasing numbers of people on fixed-term contracts or employed on a day rate on a project by project associate basis. This can be a win for both sides, offering the freelancer a higher than average salary per day in compensation for a less stable income and the option to work just part of the year, while employers get the chance to rent the pick of the specialist talent in a just-in-time fashion, without needing to provide job security.

The number of small businesses and micropreneurs has also been growing. I was astounded to discover that 95 per cent of the business done in the UK is carried out by small to medium-sized businesses.[8] These little firms are what keeps the economy running and they provide the majority of employment. The recent growth in businesses reflects a changing aspiration to be one's own boss, and again, technology and a potential to reach a global audience have made this opportunity one that many want to take advantage of.

Key: In this climate, it is particularly important for freelancers and micropreneurs to make career decisions based both on the market for their offer and their capability to provide a really high-quality product or service. Self-knowledge and a clear career plan can make all the difference between success and failure.

Working environments that work

Aside from the beach in Bali, there's a larger discussion to be had about workplace design. Workplaces and their rhythms were built by men for men. In her book, *Invisible Women*, Caroline Criado Perez captures the vast array of designs in our environment that were made only for the male of the species.

In the workplace the campaign for greater flexibility of working time, working location and the democratization of access to opportunities may have been led by women. Yet in fact, the need for crèches in the workplace, more flexible

---

6   https://www.mckinsey.com/featured-insights/employment-and-growth/independent-work-choice-necessity-and-the-gig-economy

7   https://www.ons.gov.uk/employmentandlabourmarket/peopleinwork/employmentandemployeetypes/articles/trendsinselfemploymentintheuk/2018-02-07

8   https://www.gov.uk/government/news/micro-business-boost-will-transform-the-economy–2

working hours and a humane working style would be of benefit to everyone, and certainly not just to working mums as a subsection of the workforce.

Lastly, we want to work in workplaces we can be proud of. Mission and values have become more important criteria for many professionals. We have become less tolerant of unacceptable working practices, with signatories to modern slavery agreements, commitments to flexible ways of working and investments in employee well-being demonstrating the value of being an employer of choice.

Like the dodgy sneezers of yore, we have come to expect something different. More folk are looking to work in companies and environments that support and nourish us, where our rights are respected and our mental, emotional, sensory and physical health is of genuine importance. Workplaces where we are trusted to have autonomy over our key activities, and to perform them when appropriate in our own time, space and geography.

Now, where did I put that hanky ...?

Key: Aspiration about what makes a successful and happy workplace is shifting. While status and commercial success remain one way of keeping score, interesting work that we believe in, done on our own terms and that fits around other aspects of our life, is becoming more important than ever. Companies that want to keep talent need to know about which of these levers matter most to each individual.

In conclusion

Employers...

We now need to be much closer to their employees – to understand what they want out of their career. They need to increase their flexibility in hours, working style and even what career shifts may be possible internally. Being aware that a wealth of choice remains for those with marketable, transferable skills, they could consider offering education to retrain and thus retain key talent with an interest in something new. At the very least, clarity in the career conversations of each of your key people is a powerful engagement lever for both retention and the battle for talent.

As individuals...

It is critical that we understand that agility is our key skill. We need to know what we bring and where we add value, but be flexible about where and how we do that – and what we call that job. We have the wonderful opportunity to design a role that really suits who we are and fulfils our definition of thriving, both inside and outside work. To do this, we need both self-knowledge and a strong sense of ownership to drive this forward and ensure a role that fits us like a glove.

This book is designed to help you address these issues and make the most of the opportunities they present. Whether you are working in a large firm and are interested in keeping your best people in-house and onside, or if you are a coach wanting to support individuals to find career fulfilment and clarity, this book is your road map. I'm going to show you a simple model that will transform your conversations and thinking, and help you have the edge in empowering your people to own their career. I'll share with you how we have used these methods to transform lives in companies such as Amazon, Mastercard, Savills and The Open University and give you the tools to use the Career Equation® to help 121 clients and set out an empowering careers agenda and strategy within your organization.

3 The Career Equation®: defining success in your career

I was chatting with the other half earlier this week. We were discussing peak experiences. He was describing the challenge of ski mountaineering and the satisfaction of traversing the Matterhorn. I cannot bear to be either cold or uncomfortable, so his motivation for this kind of experience is bewildering to me. I asked him why he chose to stretch his endurance and stamina to the limit to climb a mountain and he said, 'because they are there'.

For Peter, the experience of taking deep and rigorous care to learn a skill, train hard for it and master it generates a deep sense of satisfaction. It requires a level of precision, persistence and attention to detail, together with tenacious problem-solving. This pleasure in the challenge and the detail translates over to his work.

He's a sculptor.

On the other hand, my peak experience was on the open mic stage at Glastonbury. I'd found myself invited up to replace the last singer on the micro-phone. It was 2005, the year of the 'great flood', so I was wearing a one-piece rubber suit and looked like a drowned rat. Yet there was a moment, as I got up on stage and nodded to my fellow musicians, that transformed into magic. I'd started a simple blues tune, inspired by the consequences of the wet weather, and as the band fell into step I led the audience into a rousing chorus … 'Glastonbury, brought me to my knees … I was stumbling round in flip-flops, cos I brought no wellies …' The crowd roared. I felt exhilarated by this exchange of energy and connection from the stage to the appreciative listeners.

I'm a facilitator and writer who dreams of having a talk show.

Why do you go to work?

This book is about the importance of knowing what success means to you and to your colleagues and clients. When each of us takes ourselves into work, we do so not just to pay the bills or to do a great job at the tasks of the day, week or month. Of course, these things are important. But more than that, we go to work to enjoy seeing ourselves grow, evolve and learn, and to create a future that demonstrates some progression from our past. We go to create a sense of self and identity, to experience accomplishment, to have social interaction and structure in our day. The global COVID-19 pandemic resulted in many people being furloughed, with their work and trading temporarily suspended. I'm curious to know what all those people discovered about why they work and what work offers them apart from the exchange of expertise, time and value for money.

A useful exercise for uncovering what matters, is the one that began this chapter. Though neither experience we described forms part of our day-to-day working lives, both these descriptions of key moments in our leisure life offered important insights into the kinds of experiences we most crave. This, for me, is the most important aspect of defining success. Try it at home and see what you learn about the other person.

> Erica's favourite question:
>
> What kinds of experiences are you really looking for in your work?

What do we mean when we talk about career success?

From an early age, we're bombarded with a loud range of voices telling us how to define success. The media, our peers, parents, educators, partners, employers – they all have a view of how success should be defined and measured, and they probably aren't shy about telling us what that is!

Think about the people, opinions and trends that influenced your career decision making. Maybe you chose your career to keep your parents happy. Maybe you defined success by what you saw in celebrity culture. Maybe a mentor or teacher took a personal interest in you that shaped what career steps you took at a critical juncture. Somewhere in there was the voice inside, that had a view on what matters most to you. This can be hard to hear.

I've experienced the ill effects of a poor career choice many times in my work. The client who went into finance, despite having no genuine interest in it, to impress his dad and win his approval. The students I worked with in India for whom it was an extraordinary leap to feel they had permission to pursue a career in the creative industries. The talented linguist who followed her family into engineering, even though her natural talent was for the liberal arts, but her background favoured the security that 'hard skills' were perceived to bring.

All of these folk experienced a deep inner dissatisfaction caused by a misalignment between what made them soar and the work they chose. This took the form of stress, depression, burnout, anxiety and doubt. The work I do is about giving yourself permission to be who you are, like what you like and focus your attention on making a contribution to the world through choosing work that aligns with that.

> How do you define success?
>
> Who influenced your view?

As humans, we are meaning-making machines. Each of us is unique in the way we create that meaning and in what has meaning for us. We all want to have a sense that the 80,000 hours or so we might spend of our lifespan at work matter to us.

Getting to know you ...

There's been plenty of good work on our drivers and aspirations. A huge range of psychometrics, strength finders and interesting personality profiles have been devised to help us better understand ourselves. These divide into those that help us find our strengths and devise a career built around them, and those that identify our motivation, purpose or drivers – the 'motor' that powers the engine of our motivation to get up and go to work. Examples include StrengthsFinder, MBTI, Career Anchors and the Enneagram.

These tools can be very helpful to provide a steer on direction and key skills, helping to reduce feelings of being overwhelmed when it comes to decision making. It is also valuable to do some independent thinking about your unique design and aspirations.

We know that fulfilment comes from the combination of using our skills and strengths in an area that is motivational and meaningful for us. We could say that this fulfilment is what we call 'success'.

This is why, although these tests can help us to identify who we are and what matters to us, what they don't always help us see is how to combine these factors to take action on our own behalf. And it is self-knowledge plus action that ultimately leads to a life we want to lead, doing work that we want to do. If we want a career that excites and engages us, we need to be pro-active about exploring where and how we could find it.

> The most misleading idea I picked up over the course of my education was that success is the result of intelligence. It's not: success is the result of doing things. This seems so obvious now I can't believe no one drummed it into me at school. Consequently, I never did an internship or attempted to get myself elected to a prestigious student body. I vaguely assumed good grades would transform themselves into a good job the way good A-level results metamorphosed into a place at university.
>
> James Marriott in *The Times*, 2020

Each of us will define success differently depending on how we measure it. This is gauged by what we prioritise, prize and value. It's important that we have a framework to explore what matters to our people and to understand what success means for them so we can adapt our approach to development and feedback as coaches, managers and mentors to best suit the person in front of us.

So how do we work this out?

Over and over again, data sets confirm that the top scoring definitions of success and fulfilment at work are not money, seniority or status. This is surprising

Defining success in your career **23**

because an awful lot of attention is given to these in careers. In fact, many assume that a 'successful career' can only be achieved with high levels of all three.

In fact, most engagement data reveals that the top scoring drivers of satisfaction are:

- more opportunities to do what I do best
- interesting and meaningful work
- flexibility, autonomy and agency in when and how I work.

These are complicated and sophisticated considerations. Why? Because they are personal. All of us will use our different skills and consider interesting and meaningful work to be something different, depending on what we like and have an interest in. Imagine if I asked you to define your ideal holiday or your dream home. We would all have a slightly different, or maybe wildly different answer. The same is true for careers.

What do we mean when we talk about a 'career'?

I'll shortly introduce you to the model at the heart of this book, but first, let's take the opportunity to clarify our terms.

I define a career as 'a series of choices to explore how to align our gifts with how we make our money and how we spend our time'.

Notice that this definition makes no reference to progression, status or specialism. It is purely focused on the personal journey an individual undertakes to explore and fine tune the right combination of time spent, money earned and skills used. This is important because job roles and job titles are proliferating to the extent that it is no longer meaningful to make a decision about a profession that you will pursue throughout your working life. Instead, if we see a career as a tightrope, we have more of a true sense of what it takes to keep ourselves on course – exploring the balance between our work and the other important aspects of our lives, like our relationships, health, social contribution and other interests and hobbies.

Why do we need a career equation?

Whether you are a manager, coach or learning practitioner, you will know that one of the most important aspects of career management is putting the right person into the right role. So far in this chapter, we have learned that the definition of 'right role' depends on a personal perspective – combining the person's skill set with the factors that drive their motivation and satisfaction.

But why create one model for this? What's the point? What does the Career Equation® bring that all the other good tools, plus a chat with a caring boss, do not yet accomplish?

Reason 1: Fill the gap

A career is an emotional topic. The answer to the question 'what do you do?' is loaded. We can use our career to define our status, to provide financial security and affirm our identity.

Yet most of us fell into our careers rather than chose them.

This can work well to begin with. If we are lucky, we fall into something that we enjoy and are good at. But more often than not we muddle through. This is problematic for a business because we don't want people in the wrong role, doing mediocre work. And it is problematic for an individual because we spend a lot of time at work and we want that time to count and we want to feel good about what we do.

Certainly, careers advice and career conversations are not new. They've been about for a while. There is even a governing body for careers professionals, the Career Development Institute. Yet stop for a moment to consider your own experience of careers advice. I'm willing to bet good money that it was patchy at best.

Why? Because the school educational system does not currently measure its success by the career destinations and employment of its students. It is not designed to focus on helping students make the link between their educational interests, personality and skills and the world of work. This leaves a crucial connection gap between self-knowledge and employment opportunities. So we make our best guess and stumble through, choosing careers based on the roles we know of, advice from outside or perhaps connections and opportunities made by our family or other life networks.

Provision of careers advice in education is a government policy issue and the Connexions service was brutally slashed and burned in 2010. Higher education is currently under pressure to track the employment destinations of alumni and to increase their employability, but in my view this is too little too late. By the time we have graduated (if we graduate), we may already be way off course from where our unique personal design ought to find us in the workplace.

Since then, there has been a huge range in both quality and quantity of careers advice across education, and certainly no leading model or approach has been devised and adopted for a level of consistency.

Even at university, most careers advice was, until very recently, focused on professions and roles and their graduate application schemes. As the aspiration of graduates has moved more towards entrepreneurship, we have seen a shift in this provision, with more career coaches as opposed to careers advisers being hired by the top universities.

In the workplace, the responsibility for career management and career conversation also falls between a few stools. Is it the job of the human resources business partner (HRBP), alongside their contract management and performance management support functions? Or perhaps it should be the Head of Talent who uncovers career direction and motivation? Or maybe the manager? And even if we knew who it was, what kind of framework should they be using for career conversations? The Career Equation®, with the advice and support around it for managers and individual professionals, provides a very clear framework for these conversations across the business, while also skilfully managing some of the more daunting aspects that can put managers or internal coaches off starting the conversation. Crucially, for large organisations, this consistent approach can be scaled up and replicated.

Lastly, the Career Equation® provides a consistent structure for independent career coaches. There has been a boom in interest and investment by individuals looking to make a career shift. With this comes the opportunity to specialise. The Career Equation® equips independent coaches with a robust framework for exploring career decisions with their clients and some very practical tools for moving the conversation into action.

Reason 2: One ring to rule them all

Think about your management population in your organization. Do you think that all managers would feel equipped to carry out a quality career conversation?

Exactly.

In fact, sensitively exploring what matters most to your employees might feel quite countercultural to this population.

For a whole lot of reasons, managers' interpersonal skills are varied. In addition, their core training may have been focused on the more technical aspects of delivery in their industry. Even in manager development programmes, conversational skills for career coaching rarely make it into the final cut.

This is a shame because we know that the relationship with the manager is one of the keys that determine how long talent stays in your organization.[1] There's a common-sense reflection that people don't leave organizations, they leave bosses. What if every manager had the confidence and competence to have high-quality career conversations, offering care, interest and guidance to help talent make the most of their moves within the business?

In order to fully realise the benefits of this, you need one ring to rule them all. One simple model or framework for this conversation that can easily go viral and be adopted across the business in a consistent way. Then you know the conversation and insights can travel with a person across your company and you can compare the various individuals suited to a role using the same criteria and lens.

So, how do we fix this? We develop a simple structure that can be easily explained and actioned, and communicate this to the manager. This then enables a whole academy group or a whole university or a whole multinational organization to

---

1 https://news.gallup.com/businessjournal/106912/turning-around-your-turnover-problem.aspx

have the same kind of conversation, using the same language and the same line of dialogue, thus creating a consistent form of the conversation across the entire population. In addition, we teach the same method to every individual employee so that they have the self-insight to be in charge of their career. The Career Equation® thus produces a high level of clarity about an individual that can 'travel' across the business and even benefit them beyond their time with that employer. And as a business, it helps to have just one model or approach so we can scale it. Imagine if there were ten different systems for compiling expenses or managing performance. It would be so confusing. One consistent model enables a business to quickly scale up the volume of high-quality career conversations. The Career Equation® achieves this for any business that adopts it.

Reason 3: Time is short

I hate to break it to you ... but no one but you is genuinely interested in the comprehensive insights of your 30-page personality profile.

The information age has made us impatient. We want our answers at the touch of a button. Our patience and attention have been reduced. So, in spite of the valuable self-insight we get from personality profiling, we still need a succinct way to articulate our career desires and aspirations to another person, be that a recruiter, coach or manager. What if you had a very quick and effective way to develop a concise and specific 'elevator pitch' that lets other people know the value and expertise you can bring and the way to get the most out of you? The Career Equation® delivers just that.

As a company, you want to be able to quickly review the available information about your existing and potential talent pool – their aspirations and skill sets – and make good hiring decisions based on this insight. Your growth depends on having the right talent in the right roles.

As a manager, you want to be able to make the most of the person in front of you. When you deeply understand their current interests and strengths you can use this insight to enhance performance and deliver bottom line results for the team you work in. Your success depends on leveraging the ability of others.

As a coach, you want to be able to laser in on what makes your coaching client tick and what they most want to shift to experience maximum fulfilment in their career. Your reputation depends on being able to deliver results and shifts.

Reason 4: Decisions, decisions ...

There are a lot of factors at play when we make a decision about a career. And as you now know, everyone has a different set of success criteria in their heads when they consider a career move or a career decision that they need to make.

There can be a lot at stake when we consider a promotion, pivot or career change. Coaching clients can easily become overwhelmed by choices. They may respond to this in a variety of unhelpful ways, including impulsively leaping from one role to the next without due thought, finding themselves in an ill-fitting job that costs them and their employer, or surprising you with a resignation based on a 'grass is greener' offer.

Ideally what we want to do is reduce the parameters and structure their thought process so that they can make better, more confident, lasting decisions that serve them and the business they currently work in.

I want your coachees to not be overwhelmed by choice. We want them to feel empowered to take the right action for them through a scaffolded thought and career design process that is personalised to their unique qualities and aspirations. To help you and them sort out all these different considerations, you need a model that puts each criterion in a different basket. When they are clear, they are better able to sift options, make good decisions and see what needs adjusting to enhance their satisfaction or progress to the next stage in their career in your business.

The good news? Whatever the age, seniority or industry they work in and whatever choice it is they need to make, the Career Equation® will help them quickly discern what is right. Ultimately, you will also empower them with the ability to think through and navigate career moves and career decisions for the entire duration of their career, even if this spans industries in which you and they have limited experience.

Reason 5: Make an accurate diagnosis

When the shape of work and the shape of the person are out of alignment, there is a system malfunction. For an individual coachee this takes the shape of dissatisfaction, depression, anxiety, burnout. These are often accompanied by underperformance and unhappiness. For an organization, this can be costly – as the wrong person in the wrong place or an unhappy employee can prove detrimental to results and ultimately toxic to a team or company brand. Their negative experience may lead to a lack of advocacy for your company too, reducing the talent pool you have access to.

One of the challenges of this tricky situation is that it can be hard to know exactly where things have gone wrong. Like any other system, you need to be able to check out the connections and component parts to find the disconnect. This is where the Career Equation® can prove invaluable. By categorizing the four key elements that drive satisfaction or dissatisfaction – namely the environment, the use of one's skills, the subject area or industry and the values that define success – we can quickly identify the problem and work together to solve it. The solution can be very simple sometimes: a small adjustment in working hours say, or swapping a set of tasks in one role for a more suitable set in another. Trickier are the environmental factors that carry some sensitivity, like struggling with a boss's management style or the ethos of a business shifting after acquisition by a larger firm.

However, as Fritz Perls said, 'awareness is often curative'. Knowledge is power: once we have been able to define what isn't working, we can begin to build a strategy to put it right and make some role adjustments. In most cases, the strategy is either accept the challenge completely as something you are prepared to compromise on, work to change or amend it, or leave the company.

Whether you want to retain the top ten talent crucial to your succession planning, or help an independent client recalibrate what matters most to them in their work and thus aid their decision making on next steps, the Career Equation® offers powerful insight and a quicker and more apt solution.

Reason 6: The seasons turn

Our definition of what we want is unique and it evolves over time. If you think about what mattered most to you a decade ago in your work and consider what matters now, there are likely to be some elements that have shifted significantly. When I was a young consultant, I loved travelling all over the world to exciting cities to run leadership programmes. I've worked in Mumbai, Auckland, San Francisco, Boston, Stockholm, Paris, Berlin, Madrid … . All of that was great fun and a wonderful way to see the world. Now, as a mother of a young infant, I am much keener to work hours that fit around family life and to be able to work on my terms and choose my clients. As the seasons turn, so do our priorities.

In organizations with excellent tenure, it can be easy as a manager or HRBP to forget that people's priorities are likely to shift over time. The parent who decided not to take the exciting secondment when their child was in primary school may now be ready for a stretchy challenge, but no one has asked him recently. The coder who loved to spend all night long cracking the latest security issues may now want to share what she has learned as a leader and mentor to more junior members of the population. The Career Equation® gives a simple organization-wide method for checking in and testing our assumptions about what matters most to the trusted members of our team.

What's great about the method is that the individual remains the driving force. They are in charge of their career and they own their next steps. It isn't for you to identify what the next chapter ought to look like. Teaching the Career Equation® toolkit to your talent means that they are equipped to carry out this reflection on a regular basis and to schedule a career conversation with you, or update their information on needs and wants on the internal HR systems, or explore their next steps, inside or outside the company.

The more transparent, regular and frequent this conversation is, the more influence you are likely to have. When career conversations have a consistent model and a valued place in the relationship dynamic with employees, there are a number of benefits. You'll get a heads-up or a red flag when someone who has previously thrived has become a flight risk. And this gives you a chance to support them into something appropriate for this new season.

As a coach, I always aim to make myself redundant. I believe the Career Equation® provides our clients with a tool for life. It's like learning to ride a bike. Once you have that skill under your belt, you can use it at any time to revisit your skill sets, interests and priorities and make informed career choices. And though your coachees may well come back to you with their new equation at a later date to seek your thoughts and expertise, they come from a position of empowerment rather than feeling a victim to circumstance or paralysed by fear of the latest round of cuts.

Reason 7: Unleash performance

We all want to talk about our careers – but don't know how

Adult professionals in the workplace often don't have a go-to person that they can speak to confidentially about their career aspirations and their future in the business. This is a shame, as these career discussions reduce staff turnover, speed up progression and enable companies to drive the mobility of talent at all levels. As Zoe, from my coaching team, put it:

> I agree, for me these types of conversation really help to build trust and importantly authenticity. You can have the most fabulous set of values all laid out in a glossy brochure and snazzy website … but if your employees don't see them in action and feel the impact of them … they don't believe a word of it!

At my company our mission is simple. We aim to 'reunite people with their gifts, so that they can do remarkable things'.

We say reunite, because many adult professionals are working in fields where their key skills and the work they do are not aligned. We believe that when their work uses their greatest strengths, they can have a massive positive impact on themselves, their families, their teams, organizations, customers and their wider communities.

It's my belief that the future of work will take the form of roles and projects designed by specific people around their specific skill sets. Being able to better understand what each person's unique design and gifts are is crucial for their economic survival and the progress and performance of the business they serve. The Covid-19 pandemic has caused huge disruption in the careers space, leading many to fear for their economic stability and speeding up the pace of change, with expansions in some fields and enormous contractions in others. I'll be interested to discover how this plays out. Whatever comes next, the advice we give to career navigation clients remains the same.

Use self-knowledge to change and shape your life – know where your gifts are

Use the Career Equation® to seek out opportunities to practise these in your work, and satisfaction and success, as you define it, will always follow. And to our company clients, folks like Amazon, Mastercard, Savills and The Open University, we say your performance as an organization depends on each person being in the right role and giving them the ability to articulate and action their 'even better if' threshold for satisfaction and performance in their career. In this way, you can address inequality, enhance the progress of diverse talent groups and become an employer I would be very reluctant to leave.

Tears. Euphoria. Relief. We've seen all these reactions and more. At workplaces ranging from the highly technical Dassault Systèmes to the Environment Agency, over and over again, we have seen the transformations that a simple model for career clarity can provide for professional adults.

So, let me show you just how we do that. If you'd like a summary of the business case for introducing career conversations into your company, visit www.thecareerequation.com/resources and download our summary of this chapter for anyone who needs it.

One simple model can make it easy for everyone in
your organization to have a good-quality conversation
in a consistent way

Illustration by Bojan Spasic, bojanspasic.com

4 The Career Equation® model

In 2008, I set up a social enterprise called The Life Project. The aim was to help young adults live their lives with clearer direction and greater fulfilment. I started researching what the issues were and discovered that the biggest leap for young people was turning their educational interest into a choice about their first jobs. I also discovered that this was a class issue – as those with wealthier or educated parents were likely to make more informed choices that aligned their career with the fundamentals of their character. I spent five years designing and delivering my own careers programmes for Connexions, schools, colleges and universities in both the UK and abroad – in India, the USA, New Zealand, Bulgaria, Kosovo and France.

Later, I joined a leadership and engagement consultancy. There I discovered that my work in the careers space could be really helpful for adult professionals and their companies wanting to find the right fit and generate exceptional performance as a result.

I experimented with my background in personal development, personal narrative, life coaching and leadership consulting to see what could be learned and what landed well. Over a decade of experiments included 121 and group work with career-shifting mums, new graduates, apprentices, school leaders, senior partners, high-potential talent and many more audiences. Skills and passion and an impact that matters to me – it's even wider than success – it's about deliverables.

Over time, I came up with the equation in Figure 4.1.

Figure 4.1 The Career Equation®

$$\frac{\text{SKILLS} + \text{PASSION} + \text{IMPACT}}{\text{ENVIRONMENTAL FIT}} = \text{THRIVING}$$

The Career Equation® is a simple **word** equation. It doesn't spit out a number or even work as a numerical assessment. It's more about how to visualise the four key components of a fulfilling career.

It's well recognised that playing to your strengths and interests when it comes to choosing a career is a good idea. We all want our people, be they individual coaching clients or employees within our business, to work where they feel they can succeed. This might be discovering your key strength – which we all possess – or by working in an area that intrigues and inspires you. Or, in delivering a result that matters to you. We all recognise that this is key to successful performance and a rewarding career. So, here's the first piece of the puzzle of the Career Equation®.

Skills

At Career Matters, we say that people are happiest when they work in an area of skill or strength. We call this their 'gift'.

When you do something you are good at and aim to become exceptional at it you experience a good deal of satisfaction. As we progress in our careers, we have the opportunity to turn these strengths into elements of mastery. The experience of getting better and better in an area of strength creates a sense of purpose and self-confidence.

Used in the right role in the right organization, these strengths bring huge business benefits, so a win/win all round.

Passions

Passion is big in the career space. There's a lot of literature dedicated to finding your passion. At Career Matters, we define passions as the subjects that arouse your curiosity or enjoyment or even awe. You know they are a passion because you spend time, and perhaps money, engaging with them and letting them move and teach you. You might read articles or blogs, listen to podcasts or radio shows, attend events, or spend money related to studying or engaging with these.

Examples include live music, history, travel, personal development or science.

We also define passions as behaviours that provoke pleasure. These are the experiences that cause you to lose track of time. It could be learning new things or solving problems or helping others or experimenting with new art materials or playing with your children. Passions can also relate to the injustices or causes you feel strongly about – that get you, literally, in a passion.

Examples include human rights, climate change and ending global inequalities.

Not every passion will be appropriate to turn into a job. Some things are too precious to make money out of (although you **can** make an Instagram career out of photographing your children, it's not for everyone!) Other passions are for pleasure only and might be impeded by becoming a source of income – for example, creative writing or playing the piano may have a place in your hobbies but not be what you choose for a profession ... or they might be.

We will explore some of these decisions later in the book.

For now, let's say that the best use of the skills and strengths identified above is to apply these to an area of interest or curiosity – namely, to a subject matter or an approach that we will call 'passion'.

Impact

When you apply your skills to an area of interest or a passion, your personal satisfaction, sense of purpose and enjoyment increases and, generally speaking, where this energy goes, results tend to follow.

This is amplified even further when the goal of our work lines up with our values. This is what we call 'impact'.

We all define and measure our results in our work in different ways. We know that success in life means different things to different people at different times. So, to complete the top half of the Career Equation®, we need our clients to be clear about what they mean when they talk about feeling successful or getting great results. We also want to help them to be very clear about how their results generate value for a business or solve a business problem that is critical to the success of the organization they are in, hope to join, or aim to serve as a service delivery partner.

We use the word impact to define what success means to the individual.

Again, we offer two levels of reflection around impact.

Firstly, we encourage clients to define what creates their personal sense of success – which may be different to the way they measure performance in the workplace. They might feel they are thriving at work when they get the chance to travel, or to work with the latest technology or have a healthy amount of time available to connect with their loved ones. They may even describe impact as a feeling that is hard to measure, such as 'feeling proud to be a role model to my children'.

Secondly, your coachee needs to be able to pinpoint the value-add or the business pain they eliminate. Do they make systems easier to use, create long-lasting client relationships or drive engagement and customer loyalty through the use of technology? It's the answer to the 'so what?' question that our impatient, right now culture demands.

Coached well, it enables your coachee to articulate their value in the following concise way: I use my strengths in x and my passion for y to achieve z.

When you know the impact your coachee values and wants to have, you are better able to motivate them as a manager and track results and performance. You are also able to motivate and incentivise in more creative ways than just promotion, salary increases and simple forms of recognition. Again, we will explore these advantages in more detail later.

Work that is designed to have the right impact for your talent is always very rewarding. It's work they do not want to leave. Work that compromises their values or works against these success drivers can have a massive detrimental impact and lead to burnout and brain drain.

The Career Equation® can give you the insight to right the ship.

Skills + Passion + Impact

These top three elements of the Career Equation® help your coachee to identify who they are and what matters to them. This diagnostic work can be informed

Figure 4.2 Environment makes the difference

Environment makes the difference

Illustration by Bojan Spasic, bojanspasic.com

by any number of useful strengths and values assessments, insightful discussions, 360s and other useful psychometric testing.

However, they are not the whole picture.

Your coachee can have all this self-knowledge and be able to articulate their business value and yet still struggle in a job. In order to get the most out of them at work we need to make sure that they are in the right environment too.

So, your Career Equation® can be enhanced or compromised by your level of environmental fit.

Environmental fit

When a working style, culture or pace of work suits the personality of your coachee, they thrive. When they don't suit, they struggle. This is the fourth part of the Career Equation®.

The **environment** that helps them do their best work.

We say, at Career Matters, that each of our clients is like a unique plant. The plant world has a huge variety of species and breeds. Each type of plant is uniquely designed to thrive in a very particular environment. When that environment is suitable, they do incredibly well. When it is hostile to their needs, they wither. Imagine the line in the equation to represent the ground beneath our feet. The soil, in which we plant ourselves.

Take a moment to consider for yourself what environment you need to do your best work:

Do you like to work with others or alone?
Do you prefer being outdoors or in a quiet office?
Are you a fast-paced person or a more reflective person?
Do you like to work with people or things?

We are all on a spectrum and environmental factors will be multiple and varied.

Environment addresses everything from the ethos of the industry, to the character of the leadership and management and the values of the business. It includes the buildings we work in, the people we work with, the systems we use, the speed we work at and the clients we serve.

Some elements of the environment can be open to change. Others are fixed across the entire business. For example, it might be possible to gain more autonomy by asking for it or moving to a different area, but you may not be able to change the IT infrastructure!

Environment in action

When I was in my final year of a social history degree at Edinburgh University, I applied to join the Civil Service Fast Stream. I was attracted to the work because I thought the skills of a good civil servant – summarizing key ideas, consulting, writing, and managing stakeholders – would be a good match for my **skills**. I was fascinated by the range of subject areas in each government department and had always thrived on variety, plus I loved social justice issues and topics as these were a **passion** of mine. Lastly, I was very values driven and had high ideals. I liked the idea of doing work that really mattered and positively impacted people's lives. I also thought the hubbub of Westminster would be a fascinating place to work, right at the heart of things. I would definitely have an **impact**!

Seven months later I was standing outside the Home Office recruitment building on Horseferry Road. I'd been successful and was selected for the 2000 cohort, yet I was uninspired. It was a concrete bunker – and I had always loved a handsome building. I felt stifled as I looked at the dark plastic cubes you had to pass through for security. The civil servants heading in and out looked sombre and bored in their dark suits. I looked down at my burgundy flowered frock and back at them. My heart sunk.

I looked across the road. The building on the other side was all glowing metal and external glass lifts. The employees at this building were bouncing with enthusiasm, dressed casually in colourful jeans and trainers. There was a huge number 4 made of umbrellas outside. It was the Channel 4 TV building.

As I looked from my side of the road to theirs, I had an epiphany. I was on the wrong side of the road!

How had this happened? The role I had chosen suited all three of my top half of the Career Equation® criteria – skills, passion and impact. I'd made it through one of the most competitive recruitment processes in the country and secured a place on a very prestigious scheme. Yet the environment was something I had not considered at all. I just hadn't given any thought to how working culture, business uniform, style of work, level of formality or even architecture might impact on my ability to do my very best work.

I took the job though. I had a nice juicy student loan to pay off. I felt I couldn't turn it down. Though the work was very interesting and varied, the opportunities to be in the heart of government were exciting and even though I learned a lot, I always felt like a square peg in a round hole.

I lacked the diplomacy needed to get on. I didn't share the conservative viewpoint of many Home Office policymakers. The bombproof windows didn't open in the summer, even though we backed onto beautiful St James's Park. I felt claustrophobic.

Then 9/11 happened. This fun-loving wildflower that I was found it almost impossible to thrive in an environment characterised by reducing and controlling civil liberties. Though the work was interesting, and I certainly had the skills to do it well, I realised that I was never going to thrive.

Ultimately, I was head-hunted for a learning consultancy role and handed in my notice. I had lasted two years and cost over £40,000 to recruit.

Seven years later, I walked into the external glass lift and into a room of 300 people to chair an event at Channel 4. I do this work to save my clients the seven-year diversion.

Environment makes the difference

My experience (see 'Environment in action') gave me the fourth component of the Career Equation®: the fact that environment can make all the difference. My own experience taught me that an individual can have the self-knowledge to know their strengths and interests and motives and choose a role accordingly, but if they land in an environment that doesn't suit their character and support them to be effective, then they will struggle.

Figure 4.3 The Career Equation®

$$\frac{\text{SKILLS} + \text{PASSION} + \text{IMPACT}}{\text{ENVIRONMENTAL FIT}} = \text{THRIVING}$$

Just like a plant, in the wrong kind of soil.

And so, the Career Equation® was complete.

In summary ...

The Career Equation® separates out the four different elements that shape and define a thriving career. It distils the key talk points down to just four sets of criteria for consideration.

It can help you shape your work to suit who you are so you can maximise your enjoyment and deliver exceptional results.

When a career conversation is shaped around the conversational scaffolding of the Career Equation®, it has the power to change lives.

Let's find out how.

5 Making use of the Career Equation®: your career design

Now you have the nuts and bolts of the Career Equation®, let's turn our focus to how to make good use of it.

This section is dedicated to the 'fundamentals'.

The aim of the Career Equation®, and all the activities that fall out of it, is to develop the client's self-knowledge so that they have the clarity to make confident and appropriate career decisions. Clarity enables them to make an accurate diagnosis of where they are, what needs to shift and how to take effective action. For the most part, once people know what they want or what they need to fix, they are pretty good at thinking through the right action. Without the clarity, they can become stuck and overwhelmed.

The clarity that comes from the Career Equation® is defined in what we call a Career Design Statement. This design statement can help with any career decision your coachee faces. These decisions could include choosing between new roles, working out how best to refine, develop or amplify their current role or whether to stay or go. In this chapter you will learn how to formulate the design statement, by taking the key insights from the Career Equation® and turning these into a honed set of specific decision-making criteria.

For maximum efficacy, the best thing you can do with this chapter is to complete it for your own use. This will give you a huge amount of insight on how the tools work and what their key benefits are.

Let's begin with the simplest modality for using the Career Equation®.

Mastering the basics

Activity number 1: Explain the Career Equation® to another human being

Now that you understand and can describe the Career Equation®, you can introduce it to someone else. Sitting alongside your team or in a 121, explain the model to the other person. Explaining it will provide the opening and foundation for a good-quality career discussion.

To make it really easy for you to do this successfully, *I've provided a short summary video and accompanying handout for you to share with your coachees.*

You can download this for free from our website at: www.thecareerequation.com/resources

It's important to introduce the Career Equation® up front in your first conversation or even before you meet. The Career Equation® gives you both a common language to discuss the things that matter most and a contained framework in which to do so. Too often, it is difficult to reach an understanding about what is important to another person because we either lack the specific language or become tied up in too much information and insight. The Career Equation® provides the scaffolding and structure for the conversation by naturally dividing the agenda for the discussion into the four key equation sections – skill, passion, impact and fit. You can follow the clarity achieved with some coaching on what their career goals might now be and what action they will take next.

Activity number 2: Discuss the Career Equation®

Your next step is to ask questions to open up the career conversation.

I've offered some starter questions for you here, to get you going. These are designed to be open, coaching questions to help your coachee evolve their self-knowledge. You can, of course, supplement them with questions of your own.

1 What do you think of the Career Equation®?
2 In what ways does this shine a light on the experiences you have had in your career so far?
3 How would you define success in your work?
4 What's your measure for success in your career?
5 How would you describe your key strengths and passions?
6 What kinds of environmental factors in the workplace have the most impact on you?
7 Which aspect of the Career Equation® (i.e. skills, passion, impact or environment) do you feel is best met in your current role? Which is the least met?

These questions will immediately move you into a much more open and curious space. They invite the questioner and the person answering to reflect at a deeper level than is common in our day-to-day working life. In this way, they serve a dual purpose. The information gathered is of course useful, to better understand the person in front of you and their drivers. This is valuable insight that you can use to help shape the opportunities they pursue in your organization or beyond. Even if you think that you know this person well, it is so important to use the model to help you check your assumptions. What you think you know of them may be out of date or based on a perception that doesn't meet how they see themselves.

The conversation offers another benefit. It builds the foundations of a really strong relationship. A relationship built on trust, where you take a personal interest in the person in front of you, is a driver for a high-quality and enduring relationship based on care and respect. When you have this strong level of trust, it makes difficult conversations much easier to have with honesty, candour and compassion.

Activity number 3: Tell your own career story

I'm keen on the power of personal story. When you share a relevant experience from your own career story you create a connection, role model the honesty expected and demonstrate understanding. Be vulnerable – talk about things that didn't go to plan. Also share if there were any key moments or people who made a difference. Be brief but honest. Remember, this is still their career conversation, so be concise, relevant and don't get carried away!

If you have completed the Career Equation® process yourself, you might share how it has helped you to understand where your role needed to change or where there was more of an opportunity to play to your strengths.

In action: explain the Career Equation® to someone close to you – a friend or colleague. See how the discussion opens up. *What surprises you about what you learn?*

Going deeper ...

Activity number 4: The Venn Me process

Figure 5.1 Venn Me

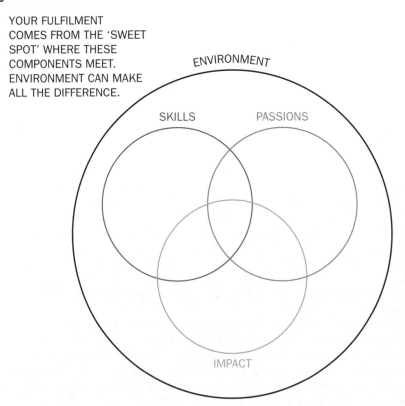

YOUR FULFILMENT
COMES FROM THE 'SWEET
SPOT' WHERE THESE
COMPONENTS MEET.
ENVIRONMENT CAN MAKE
ALL THE DIFFERENCE.

ENVIRONMENT

SKILLS   PASSIONS

IMPACT

You will remember the Venn diagram from your time at school. It defines the 'sweet spot', a place where three or more intersecting circles overlap. The skills, passion and impact pieces of the Career Equation® can be united in a process that we call Venn Me. Notice that the environment is the 'petri dish' in which the Venn diagram sits. This recognises that environment is the setting in which we apply ourselves to our work. We want our clients to discover, define and own the environment that most nourishes them.

The purpose of the Venn Me exercise is to discover the key criteria that influence your coachee's career decision making. You use the Career Equation® to help them discover their unique qualities so that they can skilfully navigate the career choices they face. They will then turn this into a Career Design Statement.

What's that?

A design statement is a succinct summary of what matters most in a person's career. It allows them to define their key skills, interests and aspirations and the value they add to a business. Here are some examples.

'I will use my skills in creativity, finding beauty and collaboration, along with my passion for curating the awesome, and learning from extraordinary people to change conformity through positive self-resonance and for a flourishing family life. An environment where I am surrounded by inspiration both home and away and can be at the heart of collaboration, magical events, work best for me.'

'I will use my skills in listening, making connections and enabling action, and my passion for working with diverse groups of people and facilitating effective communication, to influence and shape thinking, improve planning, process and outcomes, and so move from confusion to clarity. I work well in an environment that respects people, recognises contribution and has flexibility.'

The purpose of the Venn Me process is to quickly enable a coachee to identify what matters most to them in their career and be able to articulate that value in the form of a Career Design Statement.

The Career Design Venn Me process has three distinct parts.

Part 1: Venn Me – the brainstorming section
Part 2: The edit – where we reduce down our Venn Me
Part 3: Statement crafting – where we get to our first draft of the Career Design Statement

I'm going to invite you now to do your own Venn Me and create your own Career Design Statement. This is because this exercise is the beating heart of the Career Equation® process. You will not only discover the enormous value of the process by creating your own career design, you will also find the statement an invaluable tool to share with your coachees when the time comes to coach them to create their own.

The very best way to teach and use this method is from having done it for yourself. That way you know both the benefits and challenges of the process. And of course, you can share your own design statement with the appropriate audiences.

For this reason, I'm going to share this exercise as though I were coaching you personally. Pens at the ready? Let's do it!

Part 1: Venn Me

I want you to start with a brainstorm on the four key elements of the Career Equation® – skills, passion, impact and environment.

The aim of this exercise is to get a full picture of who you are and how you are made.

When you have this, you can create your Career Design Statement, a short summary of who you are and what you are looking for out of your career. In order to do that, we need to take a step back and take a 'screen grab' of you as a whole person. I call this 'going wide'.

You're going to make four generous lists to help us explore your make-up. I am going to take you through a series of questions to make this easy to do. A small piece of advice here – don't censor or edit the lists as you go. For example, you may be good at baking but don't want to put it down as a skill because you know you do not want to be a professional baker. For the purpose of this exercise, put everything down, from all aspects of your life. Later in the process, there will be an opportunity to cut out things you do not want to include in work. However, at this stage, the exercise works best if we keep all options open – so that we get as full a picture as possible of who you are.

> Set a timer for ten minutes for each section and capture as much information as you can. If you get stuck, consider what your best friend or partner would say in response to the questions I ask you.

Skills
Your first list is your skills. Let's start with this question.

'What are you good at?'
We all have natural talents, things that we can do as naturally as breathing. Some are hard skills, like mechanical skills, mathematics or thinking in 3D, and some are soft skills, like clear communication, making people feel comfortable, sharing information and ideas. What are your natural abilities?

Now another question. For this one I want you to think about yourself as a whole person – at work and outside of work.

'What would you always do, even if you were not paid for it?'

We all have abilities that give us pleasure and which we carry out almost automatically. It can be easy to discount these because they are so easy for us. What do you take pleasure in doing?

'What do you feel comes naturally to you that you cannot help but do in life?'

Write down as much as you can and ask those you trust for their opinion. This list is complete when there are at least ten skills on it.

Passions

Next, let's look at passions. A passion is a curiosity, something you care about, something that matters to you. We may know that something is a passion because you have a strong emotional reaction to stories about it – e.g. social justice or the environment – or experience a lot of pleasure from engaging with it – e.g. the arts, children, travel, problem solving. I'm interested in the experiences that make you lose track of time because you enjoy them so much.

'What do you love to do?'

We all have different interests and like to learn new things. What are the subject matters that always capture your interest? You will know them by the kinds of things you study, programmes you watch, books you read, podcasts you listen to. What's the subject matter?

'What do you like to learn about?'

Some things in life cause you to feel very strong emotions. You might feel angry or sad or joyful.

'What moves you?'

At this point, don't worry whether you want a career where you are travelling, singing, or sleeping for a living. Let's just try to capture as much about you as we can.

You will do some editing later! Again, let's get at least ten passions before you stop.

Impact

Impact is the element people often find the hardest to define.

Impact is how you define success.

We all have a different measure for when we feel successful. For me, when I have been able to transmit knowledge in a way that generates an 'a-ha!' moment, that's when I feel very successful.

I also derive a lot of satisfaction from helping people find their place in the world of work.

How about you?

So here is my first question to stimulate your thinking …

'What does success in your career mean to you?'
Think back to moments in time when you have felt on top of the world. What were you measuring the moment against? What is the characteristic that drove the joy?

'How do you measure fulfilment?'
We all have a different motivation – the thing that gets us going and really matters to us.

You might be inspired to be a great role model to your children, you might get a buzz from driving customer satisfaction, or dream of becoming a bestseller. You might get out of bed to create financial stability or love being on the cutting edge of science.

'What gets you out of bed each day?'
There is no right answer, there is only your answer.

Come up with at least three impacts to complete this list.

Environment
We are nearly there! Let's discuss environment. Environment can be as subtle as the amount of background noise or as large as the desire to spend time in frozen, uninhabited landscapes.

When you think about the ideal setting for your work, what does it look and feel like? We all have environments in which we flourish and function. The more specific we can get about what those look like, the more we can tailor our experiences and our choices to spend more time in these ideal environments.

Let me help you with this with some questions.

'Where do you do your best work?'
Sometimes culture, pace and people play an important role in our ideal environment. You might do best when you have others to bounce ideas off, feel most focused when you work from home or enjoy being accountable to others as a way to help you hit project deadlines. It is valuable to know what works for you, as this helps you to articulate it to others and to test out environments prior to committing to a new role.

'What motivates you to do really good work?'
In the workplace, we all have different ways of feeling motivated, energised and engaged. Think about what these are for you. Do you like to be in a bustling group, bouncing ideas off each other? Do you appreciate 121 time and recognition from senior leaders? Or is giving you flexibility and autonomy the way to get the best out of you?

'What's your natural work "speed"?'
I think pace is a really important consideration and one that is often overlooked. Your natural pace can range from reflective and considered to Speedy Gonzales! In my experience, the wrong pace has a really toxic impact on most people.

'What's your ideal work environment?'

Think about where you perform best. Are peace and quiet crucial or do you enjoy an open plan space? Are you excited about working for an international firm or does local capture your heart? Do you need good coffee, fast wifi or good-quality tools to be effective? The more you know about the ideal environment for you to flourish, the more you can tailor your search or adapt your set up.

Let's have five or more environmental factors on this list.

Once you have these brainstormed lists down you are ready to proceed to the next stage.

Part 2: The edit

Specificity is important. The more specific you can be about what suits you and what you want from work, the easier it is to make quick decisions with confidence or to make adjustments and learn new things. In the Career Equation® method, we do this in the form of a Career Design Statement.

Let me show you some examples.

*I will use my **skills** in finance and managing stakeholders and my **passion** for increasing client satisfaction and motivating others **to** increase profits and shareholder value and become a senior leader in business.*

*An **environment** that challenges me where I work with interesting people towards a common goal works best for me.*

Here we can see a design statement from someone in asset management who wants to move into more senior and strategic roles over the coming years.

Let's take a look at another one.

*I will use my **skills** in collaboration, management and organization and my **passion** for new challenges and continuous development **to** become known as an innovative subject matter expert and protect the business from risk.*

*An **environment** that is open, trusting and challenging works best for me.*

Here we see a nice combination of an impact for the individual – growing her reputation – and an impact for the business, safety from risk.

One more:

*I will use my **skills** in talking to strangers and my **passion** for practical life education **to** help clients find work that works for them and become the go-to expert in the field of professional career management.*

*An **environment** that is fun, freedom-filled, and where I am always learning and meeting interesting new people, works best for me.*

This is my own statement. In the underlined sections, instead of using a list of skills or passions, I have summarised them in one 'big idea' – in this case, 'practical life education'.

TIP

The purpose of a design statement is to be able to succinctly describe the experience you are looking for from your work and the value that you bring.

In order for you to create your own statement we need to reduce the content on your lists.

It works best to have them in front of you.

Let's look at skills and passions first and do some editing. I'm going to give you some prompts and on the back of these you are going to reduce down your list. You are going to be brutal and tough! You will score out anything that meets the following criteria.

Editing opportunities

EDIT 1: NOT FOR WORK!
First, remove anything that you do not want in your career. You might be a great cook, for example, but you may not want to cook for a living.

EDIT 2: NOT FOR MONEY!
Now remove anything that you do not want to make money from – you may play an instrument just for pleasure, or love wildlife, but not want to generate an income from these things.

EDIT 3: NOT FOR MY FUTURE!
Please also remove things you can do or have done in the past but no longer wish to do. Perhaps you have been pigeonholed for a particular skill set. Or you have gone as far as you wish to with a particular profession – off with its head!

Pattern spotting

Another useful way to reduce and coalesce your key ideas on what matters most to you – try to take a look at all four lists to see if you discover a pattern.

PATTERN A: LOOK FOR A THEME
Look at your remaining strengths. What do they have in common? Is there a phrase or a word to summarise all of them in one go? If there is, write it down.

PATTERN B: LOOK FOR OVERLAP
If something comes up as both a skill and a passion – then it is obviously important to you. Yet we only need to see it once in the statement, in the place

it matters most. So, ask yourself – where does this live? Is it the use of say, 'strategic thinking' as a skill that I like or is it my enthusiasm or passion for 'strategy' as a subject in itself that I want to focus on?

PATTERN C: LOOK FOR AN OVERARCHING PRINCIPLE OR CHARACTERISTIC

When you look at your remaining contents on all the lists, is there a characteristic that defines and unites them? For example, I know that my list would be filled with ways to engage my curiosity to learn new things and meet new people. Thus, I could use the idea of 'novelty' somewhere in my statement and that would feel very satisfactory.

Part 3: Statement crafting

Now you are ready to start drafting your statement. Your statement draft needs to take the following shape, so have a go at filling in the gaps.

Design statement structure

I [your name]

Will use my skills in … [add skills or skills 'big idea' here – no more than three]

And my passion for … [add passion or passion 'big idea' here – no more than three]

To [add your impacts here – no more than two]

An environment that [three to five key words] … works best for me.

We are aiming for what I call a 'messy draft'. By this I mean try to get something down, even if you know it isn't right. It is much easier to edit an existing draft and refine it as you go. Don't put pressure on yourself to write the perfect statement first time. This is an iterative process. The draft improves through repetition and refinement, so anything will do for the first go.

Now it is your turn. Draft your statement.

I _____

Will use my skills in _____

And my passion for _____

To _____

An environment that _____ works best for me.

Tips and tricks

1 **Allow it to be difficult** This process is often a bit tough at the start. Most important things are. Trust the process and keep going.
2 **Start with a messy draft** Get something down, anything, and then edit. It's much easier to rework the statement once you have a first draft. Accept that the first draft won't be perfect and begin. Then refine from there.
3 **Read your draft aloud** Reading the draft out to yourself allows you to hear and feel how accurate it currently is and to identify the amends needed. Read it to someone who loves you. Check for understanding.

Keep playing with this draft over the coming days until it feels just right. Then try speaking it aloud. Does it feel authentic to you? Edit and review accordingly.

This statement can now act as an anchor for you in career decision making.

Remember to keep refining and evolving it as your career progresses.

It's common for our coachees to become quite emotional at this point. Either because they finally feel that they have cleared up who they are at heart and claimed that for themselves, or because they realise why so many of the roles they tried before just were not a fit for their design. Whether they are relieved at the recognition or anxious about how far they are from this statement at the moment, the clarity they have achieved means you are now in a powerful position to support them to have what they really want and to do remarkable things in their working lives.

So, you are done!

And now you have a statement of your own. How do you feel about it? What is it that is now clear for you that was not before? How do you determine your next steps?

Turn the page, dear reader, to find out!

6 More on how it works

Now your coachee has learned an effective and repeatable model to discover their ideal work over and over again. The Career Equation® Venn Me process can be repeated whenever they need to review their career direction and make a new career decision.

To help inform their decision making and enable them to do this effectively, we need to put their career design through a range of stress tests.

In this chapter, I will show you my three favourite methods for making use of this statement to quickly and simply achieve real career clarity. Again, these apply to your work whatever your relationship with the client – whether your agenda is to understand and retain internal talent, or to help a private client spread their wings and explore their choices for a comprehensive career shift.

Along the way, we will hear from some Your Career Plan qualified coaches and some of their clients about the results and impacts coming from using the Career Equation®.

What the Career Design Statement can do for your coachee

The Career Design Statement rewards a deeper dive. Here are some of the key benefits the method can deliver. We will look at the use of the tools for each of these in turn.

- **Enhanced satisfaction:** Clients assess their current role and work out how they could make it even more rewarding.
- **Drive performance:** Capability and engagement increases when clients find the 'room to grow' in their current role.
- **Effective decision making:** Clients own their careers. They can explore a range of roles and make an informed decision about the right move for them.
- **Put their best foot forward:** The design statement helps candidates prepare an application and prep for interview (and test their prospective employer for environmental fit).
- **Convey their value:** Clients can let others know who they are and what they stand for in the world of work (personal statement for your CV or LinkedIn, answer the question – tell me about you …).

Benefit 1: Taking score

Your coaching client now has clarity about what their career big picture looks like. The first opportunity of the career design is to take stock of their current role. Simply put, just the insight that comes from the Career Equation® can now be used to refine their productivity, role design or skills used, in a way that generates a win/win for employer and employee.

Our aim here is to identify what's working in their current role or position. Once we can see this clearly, we can begin to coach to move their role design towards a greater alignment with their career design. This exercise enables your coachee to spend time diagnosing misalignment so they can remedy it. It also helps them to take ownership of a specific aspiration for what their ideal role might look and feel like.

Here's how it works.

Instructions

Ask your coachee to look at the completed design statement once more.

Have them score their current role against the components of the Career Equation® written in their statement.

I usually use a scale of 1–10, with 1 being 'Nowhere near my current role' and 10 being 'I absolutely experience this in my current role.'

For example, see how the statement below has a score against each part of the Career Equation®.

I Melanie, will use my skills in creative thinking, collaboration and solution-focused design **(8)** and my passion for finding innovative and practical ways forward **(7)** to enable a sustainable, impactful and valued service to the community that I serve **(6)**. An environment that is flexible, empowering, diverse, compassionate and encourages free thinking works best for me **(6)**.

Now let them talk you through their rationale for each of the scores.

What to do with the insights

Each score contains valuable information.

Anything above 7 is strong and enquiry should be made about how we could 'nudge' that score closer to 10. Anything under a score of 7 suggests that there may be a misalignment and that a better fit could be possible. Anything under 4 is indicative of a problem that requires immediate attention.

Coaching questions can now focus on how your coachee can increase each rating. What needs to shift? What is within their power to influence or ask for? What personal shift could they make? What is the consequence of taking no action to move the needle?

This exercise has an additional benefit. Where clients are taking stock of the past, it can be really useful to add in questions about how this scoring mechanism gives them insight about why some roles or cultures didn't feel a fit and what has worked well for them in their previous roles. This reflection can help to build confidence in the value of their unique design and the importance of taking ownership to find cultures and design roles that match it.

Karen Walters, an independent career coach accredited in the Your Career Plan method, reflects on what insight this process can quickly generate.

'My energy substantially increased during the session. I was amazed at how well the tool worked with the client and how natural I felt using it. The client stated that he had never thought about the importance of the environment before or the effect your passions can have on your drive and enthusiasm. I witnessed the 'a-ha!' moment in his body language.'

Wherever your coachee lands on the scoring of the design statement, one thing is for certain – they always have more to give. You just need to ask them what that is.

Are there skills they would like to further hone, passions they would like to contribute to the value of the business, impact you could harness or environmental qualities that, added to the mix, would make them feel energised to contribute further?

Room to grow

The design statement scoring may reveal that your coachee is in a role they enjoy and that suits them. They may not have a move in mind. Whether they have made a move relatively recently or are experienced in the work that they do, there is always room for improvement and growth. As we know, development of one's mastery and expertise is a huge driver for satisfaction, so even if they do not currently want to make a move in their career, this scoring system can still help them to advance their satisfaction and add more value.

Work together with your coachee to explore where the opportunities for growth are in their current role. Is there something more that they could learn about the business, the systems, the work or the people that would enable them to be even better in their delivery? Perhaps new information about different aspects of the business, or how a key section of the employee base does what they do, could enhance their performance and help give fresh insight on the work at hand?

Using simple goal-setting techniques, the coachee can identify an action that will progress their career. The right stretch, secondment, engagement or development can help them feel really invested in and attended to, as well as providing an opportunity to grow their value and contribution to the organization as a whole. We call this a **learning** goal.

If the conversation that follows the scoring of the Career Design Statement does identify that their career goal is ultimately to achieve a promotion to a more senior role, then the goal set should focus on the stepping stones to get to their next opportunity. At a large insurance client, our work with their high-potential community resulted in a diverse set of career goals to develop the experience and breadth they needed to undertake global leadership roles. These included further study, exposure to cross-sectorial projects and a deeper knowledge of a specific geographic region or market. We call this kind of goal a **development** goal.

For the Head of Talent in this business, the identification of both the aspiration in the design statement and the action to be taken next in the form of the goal, sets out a clear route map for each valued member of this high-potential community. This helps the business to identify the right opportunities to keep their bright sparks engaged and excited about the next frontier of their career in that business.

At one of the Californian tech clients we are lucky enough to work with (one of the FANG group), promotion has to be rigorously evidenced and defended. You have to present a very robust case for your progression, supported by your sponsor and advocates, in partnership with your manager. In these circumstances, the collaboration and insight generated by the Career Equation® and the Career Design Statement are crucial. These tools mean that managers and their reports are on the same page, looking together at the same target. They can then ask themselves, 'What skill gaps do you need to fill?' and 'Who do we need to get onside to evidence your contribution?', in order to provide a strong case for promotion. If the goal is more money, more status, more sales or a completely new role elsewhere, we tend to call this a **progression** or **profit** goal.

Benefit 2: From design to discovery

Once the Career Design Statement exists, your coachee has the criteria checklist for the experience that they are looking for in their work. This experience may line up closely with what they have now and simply need 'amplification' in some way. Yet in certain circumstances, the description of the experience the design statement captures will require some conscious effort on the part of the client to discover where and how they might find it.

The design statement gives the clarity to begin a process of research. The question now becomes 'Who has this kind of experience in their day-to-day work?' and 'What is their role?' They might aim to discover 'What part of the business/world would derive the most benefit from me living this design statement?'

When you work independently and the client is looking to shift industries or roles, the best piece of research they can do is to discover more about the roles that exist in their fields of interest. There are two simple ways to empower them to acquire this knowledge. They are …

Read stuff … and ask someone.

Read stuff

Have clients start to read around the industry of interest. Subscribe to journals, listen to podcasts, check out the market leaders in the new field. In addition, they should begin to collect job descriptions that are of interest – not to apply necessarily, but to learn more about the kind of skills required for the role and to identify the gaps they may need to fill. One simple exercise I often use is to ask the client to bring the job description for a role they are interested in to their 121 session. We then highlight, using a traffic light system, the role skills, responsibilities or experience. They're green if the person can easily evidence the transfer, amber if they have that quality or skill but in a different context to how it is being asked for, and red if there is a definite area for growth. We aim to remember that **all** new roles have some stretch and growth required, even if they were doing more of the exact same activities we perform now.

Ask someone

The second simple technique is outreach. One of the most enjoyable ways to deepen our understanding of roles and opportunities is to speak to people who are doing them or hire for them. Recruiters, hiring managers and more experienced professionals can provide a potent shortcut to research and a good dose of inspiration. The simple task for the client is to reach out to a number of people who have a role that is of interest and to ask them more about how they chose it, how they got there and what their day-to-day is like. They can find these folk both internally and externally to your business. They could identify them via the intranet, LinkedIn or social media and blogs they produce. Connecting with hiring managers, they can ask more general questions about the culture, the kinds of people who succeed in that role, and test for environmental fit and design statement match based on this insight.

Case study

One of our accredited coaches is the Head of Learning and Development at an international property firm. As a Your Career Plan coach, she uses all the tools in the toolbox to support a wide range of enquiries in the form of both formal and informal career coaching. She recently shared with me how a 20-minute conversation on the Career Equation® enabled a long-standing and well-valued colleague to rediscover their 'mojo'.

'My internal client has had a really successful career until now. When we met for coffee, I was surprised how deflated they looked. Their normally bouncy self was completely absent. They told me that they were considering if it was time to leave the business and try something new. Something was missing and they couldn't put their finger on it. I explained the Career Equation® and we had a chance to quickly discuss the "shape" of a simple design statement. From this work it immediately became clear that they were someone who loved to initiate, build and grow. They realised that their career so far had been three internal start-ups, where, in each case, they had begun with nothing and built something significant and valuable. We quickly saw that the role they were in had had its "mission fulfilled", hence the loss of energy. So now they know that they did need to find themselves a new challenge and recalled that this was perfectly workable within the business. They left with a new spring in their step and headed off with their normal energy restored to go and find a new commercial project to launch for the company.'

Benefit 3: Better decision making

A Career Design Statement hones down the criteria that matter most to your coachee. This puts them in a stronger position to make good decisions about their career next steps, with real confidence that these are informed by their personal success criteria.

There are some simple ways to help your coachee maximise their decision-making power using the statement. Here are some of the most effective ones we use.

1 Scoring
2 Gap analysis
3 Ask the audience

How to use the Career Design Statement for better decision making

A: Take the score

Let's say that your coachee has a range of role opportunities or career directions to choose from. They need to make an informed and timely decision about which route to pursue. This decision could have a significant impact on their career progress. Ask your coachee to identify three roles they are considering. They then create a table that sets out each of the criteria under their design statement in a separate column. So, for example, if I was going to make a decision matrix for my equation it might look like the one in Figure 6.1.

Then they tick or cross, or score out of ten, for how well each role matches the aspirations and criteria set out in their design statement. This provides an immediate visual indicator of the best fit. If anyone is interested in having me host their public interest talk show ... do get in touch – this is the only work that I think could be more rewarding than the work I do now!

Anyway, back to you and your coachee!

B: Do a gap analysis

A coachee may be interested in a range of roles, but be concerned about how well they can fill the requirements of those roles. This can be of particular concern if they are moving across sectors or making a lateral move into a new area

Figure 6.1 Scoring/decision matrix

	Do I get to talk to strangers?	Is the subject matter practical?	Does the content address 'an education for life?'	Does this advance my agenda as a thought leader?	Is the environment fun?	Do I often get to meet interesting new people?
Role 1: Business psychologist	8	8	7	7	3	8
Role 2: Dance psychotherapist	8	6	8	2	6	6
Role 3: Talk show host	10	6	7	9	10	10

of expertise. While every new role should have a stimulating learning curve, we also want to feel equipped and competent to hit the ground running relatively fast. Again, the matrix is useful.

First, ask your coachee to note down what the role description requires of them. These will form the first column. In the next column, they will traffic light their experience in comparison to what has been asked. Green indicates they have relevant experience and expertise; amber is having the expertise, but in a different context; and red is a skills or competence gap. In the third column, they document the story they would tell to evidence their expertise. Where there are 'red' gaps we then explore, in the fourth column, how their capabilities – as set out in the Career Equation® – demonstrate a good fit for this role, and in the fifth column, how they would use that capability to quickly close the gap, either prior to taking the role or on the job.

Figure 6.2 gives an example. Let's say I'd like to join the training team at Harvey Nichols …

C: Ask the audience

We work with graduates at Dassault Systèmes. This remarkable scientific technology company creates virtual worlds – simulators for flying, CAD for architectural design and simulations for safe mining and construction.

Dassault Systèmes hires maths and physics graduates with a thirst for new technology. They are innovative and curious, and their work could take them

Figure 6.2 Gap analysis example

Skills/ experience needed	Traffic light	Evidence	Where in my Equation is the evidence	How could I build this quickly?
10 years of teaching experience	Green	Been facilitating for 18 years, wide variety of environments	n/a	n/a
Background in retail/shop floor	Yellow	I have worked in retail, as a teen! Bit out of date ...	Talking to strangers I do like making matches Listening to what people need and want	Return to the floor one day per week in first 8 weeks in role Volunteer my time on shop floor before applying Interview shop assistants to learn more about their perspectives and concerns

in all sorts of directions. At the end of the two-year graduate scheme, the young adults make a choice – to focus on biology, geology, virtual simulations, science, high tech or intelligence and data systems.

And how do they discover what roles might suit them best in those functions?

As a business that has grown rapidly through acquisition, the company has a dazzling range of options. Only two years into the business, this choice can feel like considerable pressure.

Enter the Career Equation®. We worked with the graduates to define what matters most to them in their careers; we equip them to confidently 'shop' the options in the business.

'Where would you find someone like me in this business?'

In addition to the clarity provided by the Career Design Statement, we invited a number of experienced Dassault Systèmes professionals to come and share their own career history and provide advice and guidance on how to make the right decision on their career's next steps. The design statement provided each graduate with a crisp and clear 'scope' so that they could ask mentors, senior leaders and those further along in their career 'Where could I make use of these skills and have this kind of impact in this business?' 'Where would you find someone like me making a real impact in this business?' 'If I like this subject matter or I have a real passion for wearable technology, where should I be looking to move for my first role after the grad scheme?'

The benefit of this for the graduate is clear. However, there is also a huge benefit for the talent, HR, and management community. Finding out early what is driving these grads helps retain and engage them and allows the business to tailor their opportunities to learn and grow to make the most of them and help them add real value to the bottom line as they evolve.

This benefit of course extends beyond the graduate world. Anyone engaged in a career reflection process, at any stage in their career, can benefit from sharing their design statement with their network and asking: 'Who would really value working with someone who offers this?' Later in life, we can really benefit from asking our network to help us source the specific opportunities that will suit us, and we of course benefit from the fact that they already know and trust us, perhaps having worked with us previously. Those in at the start of their career lack this network, so the ability to know what they are looking for is particularly important. This process has the additional benefit of building their network and brand both internally and outside of the business.

Benefit 4: Quickly present your uniqueness and fit for your ideal role

Put simply, the design statement is an excellent elevator pitch. It is a concise description of the uniqueness of your coachee. The individual nature of the statement means it offers a clear point of difference with others competing for the same role and enables your coachee to quickly answer the question, 'Tell me about you'. This is important for advancement and making the most of the networking and connecting opportunities presented in the real world and online. It can be particularly valuable for individuals who have to try something completely different, that is more in line with their statement.

How to do it

To help them tell a coherent story about why they are making the shift, I often invite my coaching clients to complete the gaps in the positioning statement shown in Figure 6.3.

This summary can be used to refresh a LinkedIn profile, begin a cover letter or doorstop your ideal employer! For a soft copy, visit the resources section on the website.

Benefit 5: Testing the water

If a client is wanting to make a change in their career – whether it is a new team, a new organisation or a completely new role in a new industry, it can feel very daunting! Fear of the unknown, of making a bad choice and risking failing probation can all feel like reasons to stay put. However, we can empower our client to take ownership for testing out the fit of the role and the environment by putting their design statement into practice as a 'sense checker'.

Figure 6.3 Positioning statement

I'm _____
For the last _____ I have been focusing on delivering _____ for _____.
My real passion is for _____ and I have achieved _____ and advanced my knowledge through _____
My colleagues/clients tend to tell me _____
I am interested in this role because _____
I believe I can bring _____ and _____ to the job.
My ultimate aim in my work is to _____

How to do it

Applying for a role takes a lot of energy and time. To make it worthwhile leaving what they have, your coachees want to be relatively sure that they are making a good decision.

Before they even decide to apply, the Career Design Statement can help them. They can check out Glassdoor for company reviews and arrange a number of informal conversations with employees within the company. They can also speak to both HR and the hiring manager to sense-check the alignment between their design statement and the company culture and role fit before even making the decision to apply. They can even visit or shadow the team if this is logistically feasible. Discovering that the fit isn't quite right before applying or accepting a role should be considered a major win as it saves a lot of pain in the long run and still leaves them with valuable insight that they did not previously possess on the products, people and approach that surrounded the role they were considering.

Work with your coachee to explore how the pre-interview research and the interview process might lend themselves to testing fit. What kinds of questions do they need answered to satisfy themselves that the team they are moving to shares their appreciation of innovation? How will they sense-check if their new firm walk the walk when it comes to investment in the latest technology? What do they need to know about how this company manages the flexible working that they need to manage their caring responsibilities outside of work?

The career clarity achieved by the Career Design Statement puts your coachee in the driving seat for their career direction. Reducing their criteria and distilling these down to what really matters helps them to cut through the mind-chatter and see clearly what will work best for them. This detailed thinking and attention pays off when they need to make a difficult decision that could have long-term implications. It helps them to weigh up the pros and cons and be in strong position to pitch their value to powerful influencers in their network.

Figure 6.4 Navigating your career around a large business is complicated and overwhelming

Navigating your career around a large business
is complicated and overwhelming

Illustration by Bojan Spasic, bojanspasic.com

Given the huge benefits, you would think embedding these practices into a company would be a no-brainer. Let's take a look at what might get in the way of us making use of these tools in our businesses.

7 The places that scare you

It isn't news that turnover of key staff is costly. When we unexpectedly lose key talent, the cost of finding their replacement, training that person up and plugging the gap in the meantime can be up to two times their salary.[1]

These costs are exacerbated by the impact on those in their team, who may lose morale or confidence, have a temporary lack of direction, or be overwhelmed by trying to cope with the fallout of extra work. Then there's the intangible cost of a brain drain, the knowledge and expertise that leaves the business when a well-trained expert moves on out of the business without a comprehensive handover or knowledge transfer.

In the last decade, people have become more comfortable with changing roles. We all know what a precious and valuable commodity our people are, and how time-consuming it is to replace them, so you would think we would do all we can to retain them in a business. Yet, all too often, we miss out on a powerful driver for retaining and engaging talent – the personalised and practical career conversation.

When we look at engagement data, we see that the most common area of poor performance is the answer to the question, 'Do I know what the next stage of my career looks like in this company?' We know that the two most common reasons for leaving a business are the inability to see your future career path in that company and feeling that you do not like or trust your manager.

We can kill two birds with one stone using the Career Equation® method. By equipping managers with the skills to have high-quality and timely career conversations we can improve their management performance, enhance the delivery of their teams and drive retention and mobility across the company. There is a great business case for doing so and it is a simple activity to implement – it doesn't require a new operating model or any fancy software.

Yet, time and again, when my team and I first encounter new client organizations, the idea of discussing career plans and goals with key talent is initially met with suspicion and resistance.

In this chapter, we'll explore why that is. We'll look at what frightens managers off having these conversations. We'll bust some of those myths and replace them with the business case and business benefits of regular career check-ins. In Chapter 8, I will give you the step-by-step method to get these check-ins off to a good start and prepare well for them.

---

1. https://www.linkedin.com/pulse/20130816200159-131079-employee-retention-now-a-big-issue-why-the-tide-has-turned/

It doesn't have to be the manager...

It's worth saying here that not all our clients expect the manager to be the go-to person for these conversations. For a variety of reasons, the manager may not be the best person. You may have a technical environment, where the managers focus on processes and people-based discussions live elsewhere. You may find folks speak more freely when they can talk to someone outside of the day-to-day. Or you may want to offer an alternative coach whose job they are not pursuing!

Some client organizations have a pool of career mentors or coaches across the business, with whom these conversations can take place. Others allocate the ownership of these development conversations to their HR business partners and heads of talent. Still others subcontract out to us for career support for key players in their business.

The important thing is that your people **know who they can go to** for a confidential discussion on their career aspirations and that these are implemented in a consistent, measurable and enjoyable way for both parties.

The places that scare us

In sales training, you are taught the importance of tackling objections head on. In fact, you are taught to welcome objections as they mean that the other person is considering how the idea might work but is coming up against doubts that they need to overcome. Let's take a look at some of the common doubts and concerns that can come up when you start mooting the idea of encouraging regular career discussions in your business.

Myth 1: But if we coach them about their careers, won't they leave?

Careers and ambitious progression can be the 'elephant in the room', the conversation we run shy from. As heads of talent, managers of professional teams or coaches and mentors, we are used to talking about the business at hand, the current strategy and our colleague's performance against goals and targets.

It's understandable that we might think if we introduce the possibility of the next step in your career into the conversation we might awaken a sleeping dragon of desire and encourage our employee to take the leap and head for pastures new.

It says a lot about our level of confidence in what we offer in our business that we think, as soon as we begin this conversation, a switch will be inevitable!

Truth: Everyone wants to talk about their careers. If they aren't talking to you, they are talking to the competition.

While we certainly don't want to lose talent unnecessarily, it is infinitely preferable that career conversations take place internally. I'm sure you have had the experience of unexpectedly receiving an unwanted 'surprise' resignation, only to discover that the opportunity the person is leaving for could easily have been created within your business. It's a real bummer.

To avoid this, we need to understand that all of us want to talk about our careers. We spend a lot of time at work and we want it to count. We want to be confident that we have a future path mapped out and that the work we are doing is a good for who we are and what we want out of life.

Think about it. When was the last time you discussed your career with someone?

We discuss our work with friends, partners, spouses and colleagues. If we don't have a place to discuss our future aspirations in the company we are in, where do we go next? To recruiters, an external career coach or – worst of all – the competition.

Talking regularly and often about career aspiration allows you to stay close to what matters to your people and to get early warnings about any desires to move on. In addition, taking a personal interest in them and their future is much more likely to result in both loyalty and retention as people feel they are cared for and know how their future could map out in your company.

Key learning: Keep the conversation in-house
There needs to be regular conversation about careers with your team members. It doesn't have to be with you as a manager, but the place to go to explore your future in the company needs to be clear and easy to access. Remote tools and digital support are all good, but people need someone to talk to first before they access the new online training in their field or view the jobs board. Don't let that person be a competitor. By the time they have an offer elsewhere they have mentally checked out of the business, and it will be too late to try to win them back with opportunities internally. They'll just wonder why you didn't mention them earlier.

Myth 2: We can't give them what they want so why open the dialogue?

There is a common assumption that the only thing that matters when it comes to career conversations is, 'How can I get a promotion round here?' While there is nothing wrong with ambitious talent wanting to make their way up the ladder, this is by no means the only way in which people measure their fulfilment and success in their career. If you ask them, you might be surprised. They may want to stay in the same role but deepen their skill set. They may be curious about another part of the business and welcome a chance to learn more. They may be really happy where they are, but feel there could be even more they could offer to the company. They might prize the opportunity to work from home or work flexible hours way above a pay rise.

The trouble is, you don't know that until you start talking to them.

Managers avoid this discussion because pay freezes or head-count dilemmas or a lack of available opportunities at the next level, due to a progression bottleneck, means that they are afraid that they will be asked for something they cannot deliver on. So we avoid the conversation to prevent us having to give difficult messages or say no to a request we cannot meet.

Truth: They are responsible for their careers and they know it
While this is an understandable concern – it is not true! The focus of the conversation is to help them work out what **they** want and how **they** can get it. You are not the genie there to grant their wishes – you are there to help them work out the moves and experiences that will help them get what they want.

No one will ever know more about, or care more about, the right move in their careers but the person themselves. They are responsible for what happens next. Not you. Our experience is that coachees consider the conversation itself to be a valuable perk and an addition to their working experience, and most understand up front that the purpose of the conversation is to clarify and encourage their plans and aspirations, not an opportunity to pitch for a raise.

Most talented people appreciate the unique opportunity to reflect on their career choices so far and feel supported and invested in when a person they trust takes a personal interest in them and their career aspirations.

Key learning: The conversation itself has so much value
More often than not, the more you know about the person in front of you the better you are able to support, motivate, challenge and advise them. The Career Equation® discussion is set up in such a way that it helps you to better understand who they are and what works for them. It creates an environment in which you can explore together what the next steps and development might be for them and even how you might adjust their current role to better meet what matters most to them. Without this discussion, you need to rely on your own assumptions and expectations, none of which may line up with what the individual truly prizes.

Are there times when your coachee really wants a promotion, deserves one, and is ready, but head-count freeze makes this impossible? Sure – of course. But this eventuality is just one in a field of possibilities. And besides, having the advance knowledge that they are a flight risk gives you the information to make a business case and, worst case, begin your succession planning. All of which is way better than being in the dark.

Put simply, the more you know about what they do value, the better chance you have of being able to use these levers to drive satisfaction, performance and productivity. It's good practice to explore how a request made for education, development, flexibility or additional responsibility could be met, and to have given this some thought, so that if more money or more seniority isn't an option you do know what else could be possible and rewarding.

Myth 3: I must be *all knowing*

Sometimes we avoid having conversations where we feel we don't have all the answers.

Figure 7.1 You can't expect someone else to run your life and make your decisions for you

You can't expect someone else to run your life
and make your decisions for you

Illustration by Bojan Spasic, bojanspasic.com

There's a common expectation that, as a manager, we must have the answers to everything. This unrealistic expectation can censor the conversations we initiate through fear of feeling exposed or inadequate. When we discuss opening up a career conversation with managers they often express a concern that they could get 'caught out', not knowing how other parts of the business function or how to apply for a secondment role. As a result of this fear, they do not open up the career conversation and miss out on all the benefits it provides.

Truth: You don't need to know everything
Just as we cannot predict everything a customer will ask about a product or service, so we will sometimes be pressed for knowledge or insight about

roles, departments, training or funding that we just don't know the answer to.

In addition, preparing well for the conversation can help you to have to hand some of the information that it might be reasonable to be asked for, such as 'What is the promotion process in this business?' or 'How is training identified and funded?' This may be as simple as a link to the information on the website, or taking the time to identify the right person for your direct report to speak to.

While you may not have the answers, you may also have a wider network and more experience of the organization. So it may be easier for you to think through where that information might be sourced. You also have your own experience. Data points can be found and shared, but what is priceless for many is the opportunity to hear the stories and learning experiences of others. Don't underestimate the value of your perspective.

Key learning: It's ok to say you don't know
Instead of feeling you need to know everything, consider the advantage of being able to empower your team member to take control of their next steps and find the things they need. Coach your team member to be the one in charge and explore with them 'How could you find out?'

Myth 4: I just haven't got the time

There's no question that we are all under considerable time pressure. We are in the age of information, and this information can often be overwhelming. No doubt you have a diary chock full of meetings, an inbox that consistently overflows and management information to process.

There will always be competing priorities that take us away from quality time with our colleagues.

Carving out time for performance discussions, regular check-ins and career conversations can feel like another of the tasks in a long list of 'to dos' that we might never get round to.

What you actually mean when you say 'I don't have time' is 'I don't see the value and haven't the incentive to prioritise this particularly activity.'

When you think about the things that you do choose to do, how do you decide on these? Presumably they are either urgent – there is a time constraint or deadline set on them that you need to meet, or they are important – they add real value to the business: or they are both. In order for a career conversation to make it up the list and be given time, you need to appreciate both the business benefits of having them and the business costs or pain of not having them.

In part, this will be determined by your organization's culture and the value they put on both retention and professional development. Some companies have a high turnover of staff and consider this either the nature of their industry or just the price they are willing to pay. Thus they don't invest time in alleviating this brain drain. Others neither reward nor recognise the key role of the manager as a developer of people, so they too will not feature talent development and career progression as a deliverable of a manager's role.

Assuming you don't work for a business like this, let's take a look at what's in it for you and your coachee or team member.

Truth: There's loads in it for you and it doesn't need to take long
Let's recap the benefits for you.

1 **Engagement**

Expectations of employers are changing. People expect their employer to take an interest in their career aspirations and help them find their way through the opportunities and roles in the business. Exit interview research shows that people leave companies where they do not feel valued and where they cannot see a future.

If you want to keep someone who is key to your business performance, you need to be speaking to them about their career aspirations on a regular basis. Ambitious and talented people do not stay and stagnate. They want to be continuously growing, stretching, and making progress towards their goals. To keep them, you need to be in on that process.

2 **Performance**

By taking an interest, you set a foundation for high performance. The untapped potential of your talent can be identified and unleashed through a brief career conversation. Unlike a performance conversation or a tactical check-in, a career conversation looks at what the whole person has to give and helps them align that with the work at hand. Once the initial conversation is underway, it falls to the individual to own and guide that conversation in the future. They will come to you with business problems they could solve or value they could add, on the basis of their Career Equation® and Career Design Statement. Who doesn't want more out of their talent?

3 **Retention**

This is the key benefit of a career conversation. The more invested in, known and valued your people feel, the more likely they are to stay and grow in the business. When you take time out to understand their career goals and help them move towards them, you create an environment in which they want to stay. This is rare and therefore precious. A mentor manager can make all the difference to talent, and they know it. A career conversation strategy helps you build both your employer brand and your own personal brand by being the person everyone wants to work for.

4 **Succession planning**

No one likes a surprise resignation.

Imagine what would happen if a key member of your team gave their notice in today? How would it impact the team's performance and your own stress levels? Advance warning would be ideal.

Checking in regularly with your talent about how their career is coming along helps you develop a relationship of trust. This relationship means they are likely to share if a move is on the cards. Knowledge is power. You may be able to take action to retain them, but in the worst case you will at least know of their plans to move on and have time to make good succession plans.

I am willing to bet that there are some very valuable experts in your business. Losing their knowledge, skills and understanding of the company could be incredibly painful. Perhaps there are some folk you have in mind for succession. Do you know what their dreams are? When did you last check in to find out? What if they do not share your vision for their future? The time invested in a career conversation can result in a saving of thousands of hours at work and pounds spent trying to find, train, enrol, inspire and retain someone new. A little pain now can mean a lot less pain later.

5 **The power of care**

It is a human need to feel cared for. When we feel disrespected or uncared for, we are unlikely to do our best work. A small investment of time on the part of a manager can drive very high levels of performance and fulfilment.

You are the first point of call for your direct reports. Career conversations let you act as a sounding board, mentor and coach, and grow your reputation as a leader who nurtures talent.

This intimacy and insight will help you get the most out of your team and connect their interests with the needs of the business. Plus, when you get to know your team well and help them evolve, it can be one of the most rewarding aspects of being a people leader.

Key learning: Career conversations are an easy lever to pull to release huge benefits

You don't need to have more money or tech; you just need to spend time really understanding the person in front of you and helping them progress towards their goals. We all want to feel we have momentum. The investment of your time reduces the likelihood of the pain of a sudden loss of a team member and provides some of the most rewarding aspects of people development on both a personal and professional level. Many managers tell us that these conversations have become the most favourite part of their job.

'Line managers are more confident in having career conversations and have the tools, words and structure to have them. At our latest Talent Management discussion, line managers were really clear as to their team members' aspirations, both short and longer term, and I was really pleased with this discussion. We definitely were not having this level of quality discussion a year ago.'

Dawn Conneely, Finance Director, Financial Services

Myth 5: I am going to say the wrong thing and don't know where to begin

I get it. A career conversation feels a lot more 'risky' than traditional manager/ employee conversations normally do. You don't want to say the wrong thing, set up unreasonable expectations or deliver a bad news message.

It can be easy for conversations to go off track. This is usually for one of three reasons.

1 **We don't set out the purpose of the conversation**

Both parties do not know why they are there, what the end result is or what to expect. This sets a foundation of misunderstanding from the start.

2 **We lack boundaries**

We are not clear about what we can and cannot do. This sets up unreasonable expectations and makes for some awkward requests and lots of No's.

3 **We have not prepared**

It's only fair that you have done your preparation and thinking in advance of a personal career conversation meeting. Failure to prepare means you need to prepare to fail.

The Career Equation® conversation method I am going to share with you addresses all three of these challenges simply and effectively.

Truth: It's easily figure-out-able

Career conversations follow a specific structure, and with a little preparation you can feel confident about where and how the conversation will go.

Key learning: You are a coach, not a fortune teller

Your job as a career coach is to support your team member or client into career clarity. When you create a firm scaffold for the conversation, you create space for them to explore their options and interests. Remember – they own their career. Your job is to care about it too and to signpost where appropriate. Setting out clear boundaries, expectations and outcomes can ensure that both sides come in well prepared for a really good quality discussion.

You can trust the Career Equation® process. I promise.

In summary ...

1 Career conversations are a chance for your talent to think about their skills, talents and aspirations and to share these with you.

2 A good caring career conversation improves retention, performance and job satisfaction and can be very rewarding.

3 We can manage the conversation so that we do not feel the responsibility falls on our shoulders – your team members own their careers, just as you own yours.

8

For managers: how to prepare effectively for a career conversation

Benjamin Franklin once said that if we fail to plan, we plan to fail. When it comes to quality communications – whether it's a diplomatic negotiation, a keynote speech or a conversation with a child about the birds and the bees – the more we take time to reflect on what we want to say, the outcomes we want to get to and how we want the other person to feel, the more chance we have of walking away feeling satisfied that we have done the best we can to move towards the desired outcomes and be both dignified and respectful to all parties.

Let's take the birds and bees, just because it offers many opportunities to be potentially awkward (so awkward, we have a British idiom of 'the birds and bees' to avoid having to use the 'sex' word). There are a few hazards we need to consider in advance, and so preparation is key to help manage our own anxiety and do our best to clearly communicate the essentials and open up a dialogue. We might be afraid that we will look silly for not knowing all the answers, or that we may be shocked or surprised by what our child shares. Perhaps we feel that by opening up this conversation we could produce a flurry of undesired interest and activity. All very awkward. A bit of planning doesn't take all our emotions away, but it does increase the likelihood of a good conversation where our child feels cared for, heard and validated.

When you stop to think about it, being in the dark about what your teen is up to is infinitely worse and more dangerous than your embarrassment at bringing up the subject. Young people are going to be both curious and anxious about first love and their bodies. The opportunity to discuss boundaries and consent, as well as answer their questions, means you create an open door, where if they do have worries, they can come to you. And if they have things to celebrate, hopefully they might share some of that too!

Weirdly, a career conversation offers much the same benefits. Far better that you know and understand your team members and what is on their minds in terms of career, than you are in the dark and have no opportunity to either influence or support them, and may receive an unexpected resignation from someone you would have loved to keep in the business for the longer term.

In these circumstances, a good discussion doesn't mean that you capitulate to any request made. It doesn't even mean both people will get exactly what they wanted or that there will not be differing points of view. What it can mean is that both people have the opportunity to be heard and that you, as one party to the conversation, can listen to that point of view, share information that may be valuable and state the situation as you see it and offer support.

A career conversation is mainly a chance to listen well and to show that you care about the person in front of you and their interests, aims and desires. Preparation is part of the way you show this care.

What is the purpose of a career conversation?

Career conversations are a chance for your talent to think about their skills, talents and aspirations and to share these with you.

Your team members own their careers, just as you own yours; your job is to listen, mentor, encourage and advise where appropriate.

A career conversation is not:

- A chance for someone to have a whinge about everything that's wrong with you, the team and the organization.
- Performance management – the purpose of performance management is to make sure that a team member is delivering against expectations and goals for their delivery of work in the job that they are in. A career conversation is about the larger horizon of their direction of travel in their career.
- A conversation that will necessarily result in a promotion or more money – even if you feel they deserve it.
- A recruitment drive, where you become responsible for finding their next opportunity in the company.
- A hard sell of a new role or responsibility that you want them to take on against their will or better judgement because you think it will be 'good for them'.

How to prepare effectively

Your own mindset

Remember, the team member **owns their career**. They are responsible for it. No one will ever know more about or care more about what is right for them than themselves. They are more than capable of navigating their career in this company and owning their choices and flourishing, with a little help from you.

Secondly, you are in this conversation to **create a win/win**. A career conversation will help you both build trust and intimacy. It will help your direct report feel accountable, empowered and clear, and it will give you an insight into who they are. This is valuable information. Your presence and engagement will help your team member to feel that they have a future in the business. This is important.

Finally, your role. Your role is to **support and sponsor** your talent. To help them understand themselves better. To signpost development opportunities in the business. To introduce them to new aspects of the company. To recommend and introduce them to your network. And to hold them to account to help them get the things they want out of their career.

Location and timing

Tip 1: It's helpful to think of a career conversation as an extra scheduled check-in with your direct report. You probably already have regular progress meetings with them where you discuss their delivery against performance goals and where you agree tactics and priorities for the coming week. Career conversations work best when scheduled separately and spread evenly across the year. A good target is to have three career conversations per year.

Tip 2: Schedule them all at the same time. If they're in your calendar you won't forget to do them. It also presses the importance of these discussions with your team. You might like to do them with all your direct reports on the same day or spread them over a month. It doesn't matter – just make sure you prioritise them.

Tip 3: Schedule your team's career conversations separately to appraisals and performance reviews. They're a different discussion and you want your direct reports to spend time planning for the discussion, not be preoccupied with their performance grade. Imagine if the message you give about performance is a bit tough and then you turn and smile and ask, 'So tell me about your career?' This just won't go down well! Keep the two conversations separate so you can build a relationship of trust that relates to long-term aspiration, not just short-term goals.

Tip 4: Make sure you **set aside enough time** and find a private space in which to talk freely. There's nothing like a rushed chat in a broom cupboard to make a team member feel disengaged and of little value.

Optimal set-up

Communication on what to expect

In advance of scheduling your meeting, make sure that you have made time to explain the purpose of the conversation, to share insights on what drives that person in their career, and for you to provide them with advice and support on how to make the most of their time in the business. Most people have never had a conversation of this kind. They may be nervous, shy or concerned that they do not have enough of a plan to present to you. You will also want to stress the level of confidentiality they can expect and be honest about what, if anything, may be done with the output from this discussion – e.g. to identify talent or to create a skills database etc.

I've drafted an email for you to send in advance. Here it is. You can find a soft copy of this in the resources section of the website: www.careerequation.com/resources.

Dear [Name],

You're a really valued member of my team. In the busyness of the day-to-day, we don't always get the chance to spend some time looking at our long-term aspirations and direction of travel at work.

As such, I'd like to suggest we set up a career conversation meeting.

The purpose of a career conversation at [name your organization] is to help you make the most of your time at [your company's name here] so you can own and drive your career in the direction, and at the speed, that you would like.

The session will help me learn more about your career story so far, give me a chance to hear more about what you want out of your career at [your company's name here], and be available to help, coach and work with you to devise your career plan so I can support you to achieve these goals, navigate the business and make the most of your time here.

Our agenda will broadly be:

- Time to talk about your past roles and what has shaped you.
- An exploration the kinds of career experiences you would like to have here.
- Setting some career goals that excite and engage you and working together on a plan to help make these a reality.

This conversation will be held in confidence and my job will be to listen, be as helpful as I can and point you in the right direction. While I cannot promise that I will have all the answers or grant every wish, it is my hope that the more I know about who you are and what your aspirations are, the more helpful I can be.

I look forward to your thoughts and propose to schedule a 1-hour conversation on [date].

Regards

[Your name]

You may like to send a timed agenda if that suits the culture of your organization. Or perhaps you would like to send a link to one of our videos on the Career Equation® as part of the meeting invite.

The basics: your planning

Take some time to think about this person.

Who are they?

What do you know about **who they are**, how they currently feel and what they want out of their career? What do you not know?

Are there any **opportunities** for career development that you think might be useful to them? Is there any research you need to carry out to be ready?

Any concerns?

Finally, note down in advance any concerns that you might have about the conversation. Take some time to think through how you might handle it if these come up. Who else might you connect with for support and input?

Your career conversation agenda

A successful career conversation is more than a chat about what your direct report might fancy doing. It's a structured and focused discussion that places importance on achieving next steps. The structure I've offered below is designed to make it easy for you to plan and navigate a good-quality career conversation.

Key questions and structure

Now you are ready to structure and facilitate the career conversation.

Preparation documents and a career conversation agenda are all available at our website. You can also find a video explanation and an image of the Career Equation® at www.thecareerequation.com/resources.

1 **The story so far** – This is where we take time to hear from the team member about what has shaped and informed their career up till now.
2 **The experiences they want** – Here you could explore the Career Equation® with your team member. If they have taken Your Career Plan, they will share their Career Design Statement, but either way, this is a discussion about what skills, passions, impacts and environment are best for them. At this point you might like to share what you see as their particular skills and strengths.
3 **Introduce the Career Equation**® as a framework for the discussion. Say briefly why you think this might be useful as a model to think about their talents and their ideal work. Discuss the following questions.
   • **Skills:** What are you really good at?
   • **Passion:** What do you love to do?
   • **Impact:** How do you define success?
   • **Environmental fit:** Which previous roles made you feel happy and why?
4 **Career goals** – Discuss their goals. What are their career aspirations for the coming year? It's worth highlighting that this can include more mastery of

their current role by developing new knowledge or expanding their skill set, as well as more traditional career goals of promotion or new roles. Help them to identify what a helpful target or ambition for this year could be.

5 **Career plans** – Now you need to work together to figure out how to move towards this goal. You may want to use the career plan structure provided earlier. Discuss what could get in the way and how to tackle it. Remember they own this plan and should be the one to document it and set a timeline against it.

6 **Sharing ideas** – Lastly, you will want to ask the all-important question, 'How can I support you to achieve your goal?'

7 **Agree actions** – Then agree the actions arising for you both and the date when you will meet again to review progress against them. And you are done!

The value of telling your own story

In my years running career development programmes across a wide range of industries, I've noticed that one thing is absolutely guaranteed to go down well. That is personal story. Individuals love to hear how others have navigated their career and the various choices and turning points in it. Without hijacking the conversation, be open to sharing some of your own learnings about how to navigate the firm you are in, or the people and advice that made the biggest difference for you. This honest approach is always appreciated and considered valuable insight.

Capturing the conversation

By this point, I hope you have left the conversation energised and inspired, with a much deeper level of insight about what matters most to your team member and where they hope to head in their career. Documenting this conversation is a valuable follow-up action for the coachee. Make sure that they know where and how to capture what has taken place. You may have a learning management system (LMS) or people management system in which they can write up the conversation. As a minimum, do ask them to email you a note confirming what they have committed to and by when. Make sure to follow up on your own actions too.

Revisit and review

You will want to check in with another career discussion at least every quarter. Always run the meeting to the individual's agenda – this is their career. You can advise and support, but they need to lead it. You might find they're hesitant and unsure during the first few meetings, but as they get used to the structure they'll open up and become more confident in leading these discussions.

Working virtually

It might be that you need to run these conversations on a virtual platform. Here are some things to keep in mind when doing so.

- Remember to be in a private space where you cannot be overheard. I wouldn't want to open up to a whole open plan office.
- Be mindful that you cannot read physical cues quite as well online, so you might need to work hard to reflect what you heard and check understanding.
- Remember also that body language is another way of communicating what really matters. Notice when someone becomes animated as they describe their experiences or history and when they shut down. Reflect this back to them and use it as a lift-off point to explore further.

Optional bonus idea: working with your whole team

The Career Equation® is a great tool for opening up a wider conversation with your team about what success means to them and how they can chart and own their progress. You can use the model as the basis for an enlightening team discussion about what matters most to each person. This provides a great way to get to know one another better. When we ran a session like this for Capital One's finance team, involving everyone from the chief financial officer to the part-time administrators, there were significant benefits for a range of people at different levels.

Just a final note ... a word of warning

If you've been dodging timely feedback, it's time to break the habit. Career conversations will open up a person's desire to get on. If you have been hesitant about providing the feedback they need to improve, these conversations will expose this. While it is best to get this development feedback out in the open in order to either confirm that a person is in the wrong role and help them into the right one, or to correct the behaviours that are proving career limiting, you may get push back as to why it has taken you so long to say anything. My advice? Next time they do something that needs constructive feedback, and before you have a career conversation – give the feedback sensitively and in a timely way.

Remember ...

When your team member shows up, they may be a bit nervous. They are sharing something important to them – their ambitions, dreams and personal history. They may have never had a conversation like this before. Begin by setting out that you are here to learn more about them and to see how you can support them in their career growth in the organization.

Then go into full listening mode. **Listen carefully**, take notes and show you are engaged. Feel free to offer supplementary questions alongside those I have provided.

This is a suggested structure, designed to make it easy for you to plan a conversation. But remember to bring yourself and your experiences into the dialogue. Your stories and perspective can be a valuable addition.

Don't forget, the purpose of a career conversation is to support your team member to identify what they want out of work, and to make plans and take action to achieve it.

They own their career. They are the experts. With you as a coach and a guide, they can thrive in their work, we can retain and grow them in the business, and you can have an engaged and productive team who trust you.

As ever, the full agenda, questions to ask and business case for managerial career conversations can be found on our special website for readers of this book. Just go to www.thecareerequation.com/resources and download the *Career Conversations Guide.*

Eight reasons your coachees get stuck and how to get them unstuck

We know now that career conversations can be an engaging and catalysing force for good. However, this doesn't mean that they are entirely without challenges or bumps in the road. Any learning beyond our level of comfort will involve a bit of stretch and discomfort. If your coachees becomes resistant, disheartened, overwhelmed and the conversation loses energy, it might be that they have got stuck. We need to be able to notice that this has happened and offer some authentic, practical reassurance and guidance to get them back into an engaged state and not languishing in despair. We all have our inner critics and our stories about ourselves. We all experience fear and anxiety. Part of our work as coaches is to ensure that this does not prevent us moving into action towards the things we know we want.

In this chapter I offer eight insights on the most common ways I have experienced coachees getting to a 'stuck' point. I could go on way beyond eight and could probably fill another book. You will have had your own experiences of this too. Yet here, hopefully are a valuable collection of both the most common limiting stories around careers and some practical advice on how you can troubleshoot them.

Reason 1: They believe it's just too late to start something new

One of my favourite authors is Malcolm Gladwell. In his books, podcasts and talks, he challenges our thinking about our assumptions. One of his key areas is the ways in which people forge their path to success. In a podcast entitled 'Hallelujah', he sets out to explore how our assumptions about the road to genius can prevent us from appreciating our creativity and taking action towards our own personal goals.

He tells the tale of Picasso and Cézanne, artists, friends and contemporaries.

In his podcast he explains that Picasso was a conceptual innovator. A conceptual innovator works fast. They identify, articulate and execute on their ideas easily and precisely from early on in their career, developing and honing their skills in a very focused way, planning meticulously and then executing at a level that satisfies them.

To my mind, he represents the minority of people who seem to emerge from the womb with real clarity on their career goals! Sometimes they are helped in this by having parents or mentors who support them, from a very young age, to develop a skill at a really high level – we sometimes see this in sports, learning an instrument or an art form.

Gladwell explains that this early conceptual clarity was why Picasso was fêted from an early age. He blazed onto the art scene in his twenties and he nurtured his talent with a laser sharp focus on his execution. Yet, in later life, the financial value of his work, as perceived by experts in the art world, waned. You would think that someone who produced really valuable work before they were 40 would find the market value of their work to continue to increase. Yet Picasso's later work is frequently sold for less than his earlier creations.

Conversely, his friend Cézanne struggled in his early career. He was short on funds, his work was unrecognised, and he was frequently dissatisfied with what he produced, to the extent of ripping up or destroying his work. Cézanne is now recognised as an equally famous and gifted figure, yet his route to success was much more meandering. Gladwell says that Cézanne was the other type of genius, the experimental innovator. This creative iterates endlessly, with no specific end goal in sight. Cézanne was constantly tinkering with his work, exploring new mediums, and sometimes had his subjects sit for him over 100 times. He even often neglected to sign his work, considering that this would define it as 'finished' when he was not sure it was complete. Gladwell describes him as plagued with self-doubt and anxiety, often dismissing his achievements, and falling into despondency. Yet when he was ready, he truly flourished. Over time, he came to weave a truly original style, for which he is remembered and admired.

Time is the operative word here.

Cézanne's work from the age of 50 onwards is credited by art historians as his best and is much more valuable than the work he made in his early career.

What this tells us

What this tells us is that there is more than one path to genius. We may easily assume that if we don't find our direction early in life, then it's far too late to pursue a change and become an expert at anything. While this might be true for Olympic athletes, ballerinas and others for whom fitness or time precludes achieving a very high level of mastery later in life, for most of us it actually turns out there is a route of exploration and innovation that can result in deep expertise and real job satisfaction if we trust the path of our 'meandering'.

> **Perhaps it is only ever too late to make a change if we never start.**

I often tell this story to my clients because I find it incredibly valuable and exciting to help them explore what the next chapter of their lives could hold for them if they 'follow the breadcrumbs' of their inspiration. Regardless of age, experience, perspective, background and previous history, many of us will be able to craft and design work that we enjoy if we continue to explore what this means and keep taking action. Even if this is not income-generating, the activity itself can give us deep satisfaction and shape the sense of meaning and purpose in our lives.

I've found this to be true in my own life. For many years, my father was on my case saying that I was wasting time and squandering my talents. In fact, I was exploring a range of ways to bring my talent for connection and education and my interest in personal development into alignment. In the end, I needed to craft a vocation, a form of thought leadership and a point of view before I was able to unite these into a focus for my working life that I loved. This is what the Career Equation® helps clients to do: to unravel their focus and then consciously and intentionally design accordingly.

It is never too late to begin, to revisit or to realign

Reflecting on their personal story can help your coachee make sense of the motives underpinning their career aspirations. On the basis of this insight they have the opportunity to either choose again or to build on what they know and love, or perhaps, for the first time, make sense of the key values that drive who they are and what they value in the world of work.

Time *is* on our side

In an interview with Adam Buxton, Gladwell mentioned that the expectation that we should know our career direction by the time we are 18 was set when life expectancy was around 40. Given that a healthy person might hope to live for twice as long, perhaps we could allow some leeway and a little more time for self-discovery!

So many people will decide that it is too late to pursue their career goals. Let us use Cézanne to convince them otherwise.

Prescription

- Ask your coachee to listen to the 'Hallelujah' episode of Gladwell's *Revisionist History* podcast and be ready to discuss it in the next session.
- Have them research the career histories of people they admire and find someone who achieved success later in life.

Reason 2: I can't move forward and decide because I want to do everything

Many of my clients will present with a rich list of interests and talents. When I ask them if they have considered alternative careers and directions, their faces will light up and they will launch into a long and surprisingly varied list of options. About ten minutes into the list, they will start to look crestfallen, as they acknowledge that they have not completed any of these career options to their satisfaction, leading to a loss of confidence in their ability. The trouble is, everything interests them, and they desperately don't want to be forced to narrow down their options. They want to squeeze the maximum out of life and indulge their wide-ranging interests. Put simply, they want to do everything.

My heroine, the late Barbara Sher, was a pioneer in the career coaching space. She had a name for this character trait of grand levels of curiosity and interest. She called these talented people 'scanners'. Scanners, as the name suggests, are constantly scanning the environment for experiences and learning opportunities that excite and engage them. They often get a hard rap, as much of the dogma in the field of careers and success has focused on finding one niche and pursuing it to excellence over a lifetime. Scanners pursue their interests purely for the love of them and for the joy of indulging their curiosity. Scanners can struggle with career choices and flit from one to another, until they learn how to apply their interest and energy to complete each 'project' in their career journey before moving on to another. They need your help to unlock their potential through their power of focus.

Leonardo Da Vinci was probably one of the world's best-known scanners. A multitalented thinker, artist and scientist, his mind was constantly ablaze with new ideas and experiments. There were frequent complaints that his art, which he used to fund his other work, was often subject to long delays in delivery, as he got caught up in thrall to another big idea.

What this tells us

Once their energy is fully harnessed, scanners can do remarkable things across multiple fields. Your first task will be to help them recognise their unique personality type and address the limiting beliefs about scanner behaviour that they may have received from others in the past.

What scanners need is two-fold. Firstly, they need a repository for ideas and inspiration, so that they know they don't have to drop any of their options. Secondly, they need a plan and the ability to execute on their ideas to the level that satisfies them. This may be mastery (climb a mountain, speak a language fluently) or it might be experimental (learn a bit of trapeze, develop a new kind of ice cream).

However far they want to go with each idea or phase, they need to learn to prioritise one over another and apply all their energy to completion before beginning another new job. It is surprising how many diverse things they can be successful at if they apply this strategy.

Prescription

- Google the word 'scanner' alongside the words 'Barbara Sher'.
- Have your coachee read *Refuse to Choose* by Barbara Sher and/or watch her TED talk.

- Discuss together what kind of 'life design' might enable them to have all the things they want out of work.
- Introduce the concept of an ideas book or box, where innovative thinking can be stored, without the need to act on it immediately.

Reason 3: I just need a job – any job

Talking to a colleague in the outplacement space recently, she asked about the impact of recessions on the back of a pandemic and whether the Career Equation® might be a luxury few could afford in challenging times. If we enter a phase where many people are without work, she thought that people would be less interested in finding their ideal career.

While I can completely understand this point of view, I think that in times of turmoil there is benefit in getting even more interested in where you can excel and thus securing your long-term future. Plus, as the world of work evolves and different skill sets are required, we need to be consistently refreshing our alignment to it if we are going to get good work and continue to have value in the job market. This requires self-knowledge and adaptability, both of which are natural outcomes of the Career Equation®.

Are there times when it might be necessary to take any job offered? Sure. It might be true that if you need to pay the bills right now you do need to take whatever you think you can get, and fast. There is no shame in that at all. However, that is not the end of the story. Seeking out a temporary cash injection to keep food on the table doesn't have to mean the end of your aspirations. You can take the work and keep heading towards your ideal. This may take longer than you like, but will eventually pay off.

One friend from earlier in life spent six years in evening school to acquire his law degree in his thirties so he could move from social services to becoming a solicitor. He doesn't regret his decision for a moment and really enjoys his work now.

What this tells us

When I first began my social enterprise, the Life Project, I sold cakes and raw chocolate truffles at markets and festivals to fund me through the start-up phase. Malcolm Gladwell got himself a day job so he could write around it, with many of the most interesting writing opportunities being unpaid for several years of his early career. My best friend had a stint of three months stacking shelves in a supermarket when she graduated, only to find herself piling up cans of beans alongside a man with a PhD in volcanoes. She moved on and is now a therapist. I hope he also moved on to work more aligned with his passion.

It can be easy to panic when money is in short supply. Yes, an interim role might be a crucial immediate step. But this does not give your coachee a reason to give up on their dreams. It should instead be considered just a stepping stone along the way to something bigger. Everything significant begins with a first step.

Figure 9.1 When it comes to your career, where you look is where you go

When it comes to your career,
where you look is where you go

Illustration by Bojan Spasic, bojanspasic.com

'Where you look is where you go' is one of my favourite career development phrases.

It means that, all too often, we can get caught up in the challenges of the immediate situation we find ourselves in and become discouraged. Or we focus on the problems and obstacles rather than give attention to our aspirations and goals. This is a mistake. If you are going to safely navigate the twists and turns of the racetrack, you need to be looking up at the next bend and anticipating it. You need to focus on being the first safely over the finish line. The same is true in our working lives. Despite immediate challenges, it is critical that our clients focus on where they ultimately want to get to and keep taking steps towards realizing that in their lives.

Prescription

- Have your coachees make a vision board. This is a collage of images and words that reflects their aspiration for the future. It can be made in real life or on a virtual board such as Pinterest. I've found these to be very powerful for focusing attention on their future aims and goals and enrolling the sub-conscious mind to attend to their dreams.
- Remind them that 'where they look is where they go'. Where are they currently giving their attention to?
- Take some time with them to look back as well as to look forward. What are the stepping stones that got them to this moment? What do they see as the future stepping stones that will take them closer to their desired outcomes?

Reason 4: I don't have any connections in that industry

In my first book, I described the path to success of Maxi Jazz, lead singer of the band Faithless. Earlier in life, before the band, Maxi was working as an engineer at British Telecom and a DJ by night. He had no contacts or network in the wider professional music scene. By the time that he happened on a chance connection that led to Faithless forming, he had been in the part-time performance space for nearly two decades and a telecoms day job for over ten years.

In between, he kept getting out there, being open to people, connecting with other performers and building his network. In the end, success came from an unexpected collaboration with partners that might have surprised him. The moral of the story is you never know where or when the connection that would change your life will arise. So be open to everyone.

What this tells us

Social capital is essential. There is no question that people with more social capital, and who know how to use it, have a distinct advantage. It's also of critical value to our clients when they are considering making a shift. Without doubt a network in the relevant field can speed up and improve access to opportunities. A network can open doors, make introductions and help your coachee get access to new roles, doing a lot of the legwork of the first steps of a career change.

Every sector has its cliques. Some are more cliquey than others. If your coachee is new to a field or industry and hoping to make a move, one of the most valuable things they can do is begin to connect with and establish a network in that industry. Simple activities such as attending events and conferences where their new peers hang out are an excellent education in the new field and will help to build connections. In addition, subscribing to the relevant journals, joining membership organizations or taking virtual classes in their new subject areas are all ways to begin to get to know folks in the field. Many fields also have specialist recruiters with a deep expertise in their market. Your coachee needs to spend time researching these angles and making these connections.

Remember that network building works best when our primary intention is to be curious and to be useful. Remind your coachees to explore how they can add value and be interested in the other person, reducing the sense that they are only making connections for their own gain.

Prescription

Once a client is clear on their career design and the experiences they want to have in their work, they can send out a message to friends and colleagues asking for help forming connections in their desired new field. A specific request enables others to be more helpful. Those who know, like and trust them are likely to do what they can to make introductions and have their own social and professional networks to draw from, so your coachee doesn't have to do all the legwork alone.

- Make it fun. Encourage a client to connect with five new people on LinkedIn per day, sending personalised messages alongside the connection request.
- Set specific goals for attending events and learning more about the sector. For instance, have one conversation a month with someone who does what you want to do or is in the sector you want to get into.
- Six degrees of separation – clients can make a bold request and see what comes back. This could include a speculative application to the employer of their dreams or sending out a social media request to their nearest and dearest asking them to put them in touch with their ideal employer, mentor or hiring manager.

Reason 5: I will have to take a pay cut to make a shift

A common objection to a lateral move or change to a job that is a better fit, is the concern that your coachee will need to take a pay cut. It is understandable that they would think this – after all, they are moving into a realm where they have less expertise than other candidates who have spent more time in that sector. However, clients tend to forget what they are bringing with them. For example, a client moving from a large international make-up firm found herself a new and exciting role in a self-tanning start-up. These folks were thrilled to have someone with experience of marketing in the 'biggest' firms around and were happy to pay an equivalent salary, albeit for part-time hours, which suited my client better anyway as a new mum. It's best not to get into an argument with the client of course, but invite them to consider if an alternative perspective of 'who really values what I bring?' could help them to generate exciting possibilities of moving at least on an equal salary, or perhaps even more money.

It is reasonable to consider that a move outside of high finance or a very corporate environment into a more socially driven profession is likely to involve less money. This has to be balanced out by a few considerations. Firstly, how many hours are they working now? Does this then make their hourly rate less compelling? Secondly, are they burned out, upset and exhausted – in which case, the golden handcuffs are being exchanged, literally, for their own life force. Which doesn't seem such a good deal. Lastly, where are the opportunities to progress in their new profession, either in seniority and salary or in terms of wealth of experience and expertise? Not every kind of wealth is calibrated by cash.

What this tells us

Of course, we all want to be paid fairly for a good job, well done. Sometimes imposter syndrome can prevent us going for a senior role we are well qualified for, because we are afraid of failing in this new environment. To prevent money being the reason not to make the move, it can be useful to negotiate with the new employer. Your coachee, for example, could identify that they do have sectoral knowledge to gain before they can hugely add value to the business. So, they may propose a 10 per cent reduction in salary until they pass their three-month probation. This could reduce risk on both sides and help them feel more comfortable about being in integrity as they learn.

Prescription

- Sometimes it is the case that to go into more satisfying work, a pay cut is required. If so, work with your coachee to establish what economies could be made.
- What would they be willing to exchange in order to have a more balanced or fulfilling life?
- Review the efficiencies that could come with a new role. If, for example, they can work from home and no longer need to pay for the commute, and thus also gain two hours of life back each day, what's that worth? Or perhaps a new employer would support them in acquiring new skills and qualifications and invest in them in that way.
- Lastly, have the client explore the skills and experience they bring with them and put a price to their value. To the right audience in the market, their transferable skills, network or experiences have tremendous value – perhaps more value than their current take-home pay. (NB This is why Nick Clegg now works at Facebook even though he has no previous experience and the Coalition government was a bit of a mess. I bet he gets paid more than in public life too.)

Reason 6: I might not be the best at it, AKA imposter syndrome

In his recent *Art Club* show during the lockdown period on Channel 4 in April 2020, Grayson Perry said he took imposter syndrome as an indication that he was trying something exciting and new.

So often, when we step outside of our comfort zone, we go into polarised thinking that says, 'Either you are an expert and do an amazing job or you are a total shambles.' This leaves no room for the huge range of other outcomes that could result from a change in direction or role.

Remember that it's being on a learning edge that enables a baby to walk. It's essential for them to try and fail and try and fail, many times, in order to successfully launch themselves onto their two legs.

For all of us, in order to master anything new, we have to be willing to experiment and to fail. Imposter syndrome occurs when we compare another person's outer appearance with how we feel in our inner world. We decide that they are shiny and perfect, and we are in some way inadequate, and it is only a matter of time before we will be discovered as undeserving, incapable and definitely in the wrong role!

All of us, both coaches and clients, will suffer from imposter syndrome occasionally. The trick is, how do we help our clients to keep going, to make the application and to move forward, in spite of the fears and doubts about their capability that imposter syndrome might generate?

What this tells us

Fundamentally, imposter syndrome is about preparing ourselves to be exposed and vulnerable while we learn. My personal prescription is first of all to recognise the value in the fear. Fear is a healthy form of self-protection in action. We can acknowledge our fear for trying to keep us safe and then respectfully ask it to step aside so we can keep moving forward.

Allow your coachee to get really into the catastrophe story they have in their head. The one that goes: if they don't deliver a perfect pitch, they will be fired and banished to the ends of the earth etc., etc. Have some fun exploring this story and its origins and then ask the client If they think they would actually survive if they were found out as less experienced than they thought they should be. Once we realise that we will probably make it through alive, we have a different perspective. Then the next question is, how can we avoid getting into that catastrophic situation? What could we learn, who could we work alongside, what could we practise, to help us to move more towards our desired outcome than the one that we fear?

Some good 'un-sticking' questions for imposter syndrome

'What is the worst that could happen? Would you survive if it did?'

This is such a useful question to get the client's worries out on the table fast. Once you know where they go when they consider 'failure', you can work with them to manage the feelings and implement a risk-management plan to prevent the worst occurring. You can also work on the beliefs themselves by asking my second favourite question:

'What else, apart from this worst-case scenario, could be true about where you might end up if you go for it?'

A catastrophic fear about the future is just a fantasy. No one knows what the future holds. I figure, if we are going to spend time fantasizing about our future, we might as well indulge in a good and exciting fantasy, rather than a negative spiral.

Prescription

Look up the analogy of the elephant and the rider by Jonathan Haidt. Explain to a client that to master our mindset, we need to give the rational part of our mind a plan and direction (the rider), and the emotional part (the elephant) the motivation to feel excited about change and work in an environment (the path) that best suits the achievement of our personal goals. Help your coachee to take action to master these three aspects of change management in a way that empowers them to grow over time and be of their best.

Find the Reddit thread started by Neil Gaiman, the science fiction writer, on imposter syndrome. Discuss the freedom that comes from realizing that even best-selling authors feel the same way about stepping into something new. He has this lovely story where he talks about being at a gathering of the great and the good and thinking he didn't deserve to be there. He stood next to an elderly gentleman who was also called Neil and confided to Gaiman that he too felt the same.

That man was Neil Armstrong.

Moral of the story – we all suffer from it, just don't let it stop your coachee!

Reason 7: Better the devil you know

It's a key human driver to aim to avoid discomfort and seek out comfort. There are a few personality types that really enjoy the discomfort caused by challenge, novel environments and taking considered risks, but for many of our clients change is just downright scary. We can put aside the worry about the range of options and choice factors – the Career Equation® solves this for us. Yet we still need to help clients become more comfortable with being uncomfortable, because any shift into new responsibilities, a new role or a new industry is likely to induce a level of anxiety that may prevent some of them from making the move they really want.

Many clients will go into active resistance and anxiety when it comes to making a change. We need to help them to overcome the resistance, but we also want to respect the useful indications that fear of change may be giving them. After all, our survival over many millennia has depended on sticking to the familiar paths and the safe foods, people and places, so alertness to the dangers of change is hardwired into our DNA as a powerful self-preservation tool.

What this tells us

First of all, take time to understand the underlying key issues. Is it leaving the familiar team, the knowledge gap that opens up when they leave a familiar workplace where they know the processes, clients and people and move into a whole new sector, where the learning curve is steep? Is it that they are afraid of failing or that a change of employment could feel less rewarding or even a step back from where they are currently? Once you have got to the heart of the anxiety, you can work on the real issue.

Secondly, sometimes it is important to give permission for the change not to take place. So, it is really valid to question from the angle of 'What if you do nothing?' This helps to establish the consequences of inaction and the real-world impacts that the current role is having for them. It may be that, actually, these are not so severe as to require immediate action, or they may be deeply galvanizing. Either way, this is a useful assessment.

Lastly, explore the impact of empowered decision making. I am fond of the phrase 'No choice is still a choice.' If the client decides to take no action or to wait for things to resolve themselves, they need to understand that this is still a strategic decision that they are making. They can wait until redundancy or a performance issue or a team reshuffle will 'sort' the problem for them. In practice, some people do prefer to do so – this does mean that their career gets done for them or done to them. Generally speaking, the more empowered we feel about anything in life, the more mentally healthy our response is. We want to encourage them to make empowered, proactive and informed decisions where they drive and own their career, including making scary choices and taking action. To do so, it is useful to highlight that refusing to take action or consider a change is, in itself, one of a range of response options open to them. In the end, it is all about giving your coachee the power to choose what works for them.

Prescription

- Research matters. We can ease clients into transition and help them feel more confident about their choices once they do their research. How could they find out more about a prospective company and its culture before committing?
- Share Carol Dweck's 'growth mindset' philosophy. Explore where and how your coachee has previously adopted a growth mindset, believing in their capability to manage change and the value of adapting and learning as they go. Ask them to recollect another time in their lives where they made a change for the better. How could they access those inner resources again?
- Set homework to challenge their perspective and increase their sense of enjoying freshness. This may be something as simple as a challenge to do

something different every day for a week, such as read a new blog, walk a new way to work or listen to a podcast that represents a view that is different to theirs. Ask them to note down what they notice about the richness and variety that comes from change and difference.

Reason 8: They genuinely are being overlooked due to discrimination

This does happen. And all too often. Promotion on merit may fall foul of institutional and personal bias, group think and plain old discrimination. Talented people can be and are overlooked for promotion or pigeonholed or sidelined because of the most narrow and ignorant forms of discrimination – both conscious and unconscious.

So, how do we help our client to be seen and to stand up to racism or gender discrimination or whatever it is that is causing others to treat them unfairly?

First, we have to recognise where business was born. Most companies were designed by white men, for white men. With a long history of similar folk coming through the pipeline into leadership, they may unconsciously continue to promote 'people like me', excluding talent who don't look and feel familiar. Much to the detriment of their business, too many organizations continue to drive a culture that works in the best interests of the majority and excludes everyone else. Do you work in one? What do you think needs to be done?

If your coachee is being overlooked for progression and development and their perspective is that this is likely because of a point of difference, assume that they are correct in this until proven otherwise. Do your best to equip them to find the right way for them to introduce the challenge as to why they, in comparison to other colleagues with less experience or a lower level of performance, have been sidelined. If they feel unsafe to surface these issues, offer encouragement to find a culture in which their contribution will be genuinely welcomed and their whole self recognised and valued – they do not need to stay in a toxic environment and risk the ill effects on their health, confidence and well-being.

What this tells us

The demonstrable inequalities in UK employment statistics speak for themselves, whether we look at the 25 per cent unemployment rate among young men of Caribbean origin or the challenges female academics face in getting their work valued and published in the most prestigious journals. Books such as Akala's *Natives* and Caroline Criado-Perez's *Invisible Women* do a fantastic job in demonstrating how inequality is both systemic and insidious. We all need to play our part in tackling and unravelling these systemic inequalities. As a coach, you can empower your coachee to constructively challenge what is afoot and to make clear the value that they bring.

While exploring the impact on career outcomes would require the work of a whole other book, and one I would be very interested to write, in this instance, let me offer a few tips and tools for helping your coachee to realise their full potential.

Prescription

- Use the Career Equation® and Career Design Statement to support your coachee to be both succinct and impactful about their distinctive value to a business. If this is not picked up and run with at their existing firm, help them find somewhere where it is.
- When feedback arises that seems to be specific to challenging the nature of a person – e.g. 'Your tone', 'You're difficult to work with' – I've found a useful question to ask is 'Compared to whom?' This equips your coachee to gently challenge the preconceptions of the feedback giver, forcing them to either helpfully signpost to someone who is role modelling a desired approach or to check their internal bias as to whether the behaviour is problematic simply because of who is seen to be doing it.
- A community of supportive colleagues is bound to bring strength and expand opportunities. Work with your coachee to help them join and be active in appropriate networks, expand their community through education and connections, and establish allies, mentoring relationships and champions to support their visibility and navigation of the business.
- If you are an internal coach or manager, be proactive about looking for opportunities to coach a diverse talent pool. Reach out and extend the offer more frequently to make sure that recipients of coaching and development in your business are not always the same old crew. Be sure to overextend levels of help and support to those who have not traditionally been a recipient and frankly should have been. In your private practice, consider pro-bono and voluntary outreach work. We should all be called to do our bit to create a more meritocratic society.

And finally ...

Wherever your coachee finds themselves getting stuck, and we all do from time to time, make sure that this is not a reason to give up. Stalling, taking it slow, reflection, all of these are valid additions to a career navigation strategy. However, our duty is to keep them honest in moving towards what matters most to them and to help them do the hard yards to get there. If I've missed a barrier that impacts your coachees, drop me a line at me@ericasosna.com and I will do my best to suggest a way to figure it out with them that may inspire a breakthrough. I've included one of my favourite 'internal myth busting' exercises in the resources section of the Career Equation® website: www.thecareerequation.com/resources.

10 The ideal set-up: my advice for independent career coaches

I remember that in 2004, when I trained as a life coach, most people had no idea what it meant. The puzzled response to 'What do you do?' was usually a 'So what is that, exactly?'

We were familiar with coaches for sport, but the idea that you could be coached to achieve personal goals, improve relationships, lose weight, start a business or even change career direction seemed a foreign concept. It kind of fell between therapy, advice and education and led to frowning brows.

How things have changed! In the last decade, the market for coaching education has exploded. Business schools like Ashridge and accrediting bodies such as the Institute of Leadership and Management (ILM) now offer MAs and diplomas in the subject. Private organizations like the Coaching Academy provide free weekend tasters to upsell their longer-term intensive programmes, and online adverts abound promising a 'six-figure' practice if you simply attend a webinar and apply a 'proven system'.

Navigating this environment is complex – both for the new or aspirant coach and for the more experienced coach, looking for a trusted supplier and a credible model. To become accredited is a costly decision. Quality control can be dubious, and the online division of the coaching education sector is largely unregulated. Membership organizations like the International Coach Federation, Association for Coaching and the Career Development Institute have attempted to bridge this gap, providing a level of quality control for affiliated accrediting organizations. However, like doctors and other highly qualified folk, a qualification does not necessarily make you good at what you do. Some of the world's best coaches, like my heroine Barbara Sher, had no formal qualifications. This means there is still a risk for the first-time coaching client, who cannot always be sure that what they are getting is good-quality support from an experienced professional.

However, there is no question that the profession is on the up and up. There is huge demand for education and coaching qualifications and an increasing demand for the paid services of coaches. The career coaching space offers practical, empowering, tangible results for clients and a huge sense of satisfaction for coaches. Delivered well, it has a broad application working effectively alongside education, voluntary sector, welfare, recruitment, outplacement or internal talent programmes.

Why your career coaching practice matters

I believe that independent career coaches offer a very important service that addresses a significant gap in the market and in the education of professionals in the UK. While career advice can be very high-quality and helpful if you know your direction, very often the key question your coachee voices is 'I don't really know where to start in choosing a profession or in choosing a new direction.' This is where coaching steps in.

For me, there is a spectrum of coaching. At one end, you have the entirely question-based philosophy, that assumes the client has all the answers. At the other, you have the trouble-shooting and practical education end, where the client's self-discovery is accompanied by tools and strategies to help them move forward and thus provide an element of 'education' too. Career coaching, like parent coaching, sits at the latter end of the spectrum.

Like parent coaching, the benefits of investing in the insight and skills generated through an effective career coaching experience can last a lifetime, and be used time and time again to positive effect. And like being a parent, making the most of a career is a huge driver for satisfaction and also for challenge for most people. It requires a commitment to navigate and make the most of our opportunities to learn. Thus, your target audience is as broad as anyone who has, or wants to have, a job they enjoy.

The Career Equation® and the tools that sit around it are a very structured and practical process for self-discovery and career clarity. There is little more rewarding in life than watching your coachee uncover what it is that defines fulfilment in work for them.

You can trust this process to deliver the goods.

The method works for clients of all ages, backgrounds, education levels and industries. For anyone interested in our own accreditation for coaches, you can find out more at www.thecareerequation.com.

There are plenty of other schools of thought on careers and on coaching, so know that my perspective here is entirely my own, informed by 15 years of practice, eight years of teaching other coaches our method and taking notes from insights from clients, colleagues, peers and other experts. Your practice is your practice and you will design it to uniquely serve your ideal client and deliver on your unique promise.

Take what's useful and leave the rest. With that in mind, let's focus on some key elements to make sure that your work delivers the maximum impact.

Know your niche

My key advice for coaches is ... stay in your lane.

By this I mean know what your niche is, your zone of excellence, your own career design in fact, and specialise in that area. This will not only make you a better coach to your specific client audience, it will also make you easier to find and easier to buy from. I acknowledge that this book is all about the possibility of change, yet I believe when you have found your zone of brilliance, you ought to stay in it and deepen your expertise!

Here are the reasons why I think this is so important.

A. You can be sought out and build a name for yourself

When you focus your attention on a key group or market, be it stage of career (graduates, senior executives), type of transition (e.g. returning to work after a career break, moving from manager to leader), characteristic (such as gender or race, or by specialist sector area – 'I help accountants move into new professions', 'I help professionals aged 50+ to begin a new career'), you immediately become more distinctive and easier to find. Giving the authentic impression of sector expertise is how you attract the right audience and the right clients to you in the first place. It is how you build trust. And it is really rewarding.

Plus, your social media and engagement strategy is helpfully shaped by your niche. You know who you are writing for. You know what their concerns are, and you are able to produce thought leadership that is of value to that community.

B. Being an expert on all jobs is impossible

The world of work is proliferating with a huge range of new roles. To be an expert on all these roles is impossible. Finding a focus by industry, sector or 'personality type', e.g. technical experts, helps you to focus your attention and expertise on a particular field of knowledge. You will get to know the journals that relate to that industry, the membership organizations, how business is done and talent sourced, who the main recruiters and big players are. This makes you much more valuable to your coachees.

C. You know their struggles better

The community you choose will look to you for understanding of their struggle. They will want to hear stories of success that give them hope that they too can make the leap they dream of. They want to benefit from your network, advice, education and experience. They want your story to be relatable to them. The more you can share stories, case studies and tools that relate specifically to your audience, the more valuable you are to them.

D. One ring to rule them all

Imagine if you said you serve everyone from young adults leaving education to senior leaders in corporates. How would you put together your marketing material? How would you speak to all these audiences? How would you explain your different price points? You can see how this would quickly become messy and hard to illustrate clearly. Niching allows you to set out one stall, one process, and to iterate over and over so you develop a phenomenal process that delivers deep expertise and quick, impactful results. Which in turn gives you new case studies and stories to share, thus increasing your credibility and winning over new audiences.

How to decide on your niche

Simple. Use your career equation. Identify what gives you the most joy. What do you know the most about? My comedy teacher, Gill Edwards, used to always encourage us to draw from our own unique experiences and history to establish our own comedic style. I think this is good advice for career coaches too. You are often very effective when you coach to an industry you know and understand. Equally, you can choose a niche that relates to your own life experience. I could choose to focus on people moving from private to public sector, or new mums who want to set up their own business. Or women of colour in the professional services field. All of these relate to my own characteristics and experience.

I'm all about lifelong learning and have had multiple careers of my own. I decided to focus my career coaching practice on coaching people on crossroads at 45 and above. The world around us is changing fast, as we move from a three-stage life in which we educate, work and retire, to a multi-stage life where lifelong working and reinventing your career on a regular basis will be the new normal. If we all need to work around 50 instead of 40 years this means that when you hit your midlife years you have still another 25 to 30 years of working ahead of you. I love to help others find the way to make the most of this time.

Nicolette Wykeman, Midlife Career Coach
www.silverforcecoaching.com

I chose my niche because it's something I already do in my life. I live it and I breathe it, therefore it made sense to me to be able to coach on it! I'm a co-parent coach. I developed The Co-Parent Way™ and I coach parents who are separating on how to redefine their relationship so they can bring up their child together. Keeping the parental bubble as whole for their kids as possible is really important for a child's healthy cognitive development. I do lots of other coaching too, but this is the area I'm interviewed about, I write about and am consulted on.

Marcie Shaoul, Director of Rolling Stone Coaching
and founder of The Co-Parent Way™

When it comes to my niche, I work predominantly with mature professionals looking at transitioning in their career to something new, or they feel stuck and are finding it hard to move forward. They may be struggling to break through and have the visibility and impact they want. This feeling of 'being stuck' can come in a number of guises from fear, anxiety, overwhelm, frustration, lacking confidence and many more. I have coached many people through whatever form of career transition they are facing and so it's the area of career coaching that I have most knowledge and expertise in. I've been there personally too, changing sectors twice during my time, so have great empathy and understanding for my client's situation.

Zoë Schofield, career coach and career consultant

I am a mediator. I am a coach. I am passionate about human relations. My quest has become my niche: to empower businesses and people to relate harmoniously with one another, so they can live peacefully with their differences, and free from the strains of discord.

Over the years, I have coached businesses to disentangle from commercial disagreements, recognise value in one another, restore their relationships and continue marching side-by-side doing business that is mutually beneficial to them.

On a more personal level I help people discover value in themselves and others, so they uncover their talents, build strong bonds and manifest positive-transformative-collaborative outcomes.

In the workplace, this generates trust, loyalties and synergies in support of meaningful careers and successful businesses. People benefit from it. Businesses benefit from it.

Luciana Vargas, mediator and coach

Establish your offer

Know what works for you and for your audience. Early on in your career this will be an iterative process, experimenting with what works through a process of trial and error. Over time, you will come to know what works best for you and gets the best result for your coachees. You may deliver some knowledge content up front, in the form of a video or ebook. You might find effective ways to automate pre-work and enrolling into your coaching. You will define how best to make use of automation, online resources, technology and in-person time to deliver the ideal experience for your coachee.

Think carefully about pricing. You need to be mindful of the current rate for your chosen audience and to align this with the hours you want to be working. It's important that you know your worth and what your audience considers to be good value. My encouragement if you are new to the field is to build upwards from an average day rate. Going in at a silly fee with little experience is going to make you feel under pressure and is just not fair to your coachees. Respect and expertise must be earned. They can't be falsified through high fees.

Finally, be clear on your deliverables. What will a client get from you in addition to your time? More education? Templates? A review of their CV? Be sure to list out what is to be expected and contract accordingly. As in any professional situation, it is much better to underpromise and overdeliver than the other way round!

What is the promise to the client?

I believe a good coach always aims to empower their client so much that they make themselves redundant in the process as quickly as possible.

Bearing this in mind, what is your customer promise? Where can they expect to be by the end of the process, assuming both of you put the work in?

For example, in my own coaching practice, I've learned that the six-session Your Career Plan process delivers real results. As long as both I and my coachee do our homework and keep up the momentum, you can reasonably expect to be heading towards a final interview for a new role by the time our journey is over. While the speed and time frame for how these sessions roll out is theirs to decide, I know that the process works and can clearly explain what happens when and why.

One thing I promise up front is that, if they are nearly there but not quite when our six sessions are up, I will give them the extra time needed to help them get over the line, at no extra cost. This provides reassurance and confidence on both sides. The client knows their investment will not be wasted and that they will not be left hanging. Plus, I get to ensure that their outcome is as successful as possible, which is a win/win all round.

However, I only make this offer once we have had a call to check chemistry and compatibility – I want to make sure I can keep the promise, which means I need to be certain that I can help them and am the right fit for them.

All about the chemistry

Chemistry is crucial to a successful coaching assignment. Personally, I never take on a coachee without a chemistry call. And I always recommend that they speak to more than one coach, even if they feel pretty sure that they want to work with me. Coaching is an investment of time, money and energy and it's important you are confident that your coachee is a fit and that they feel able to trust you and go deep quickly.

You'll evolve your own process for a chemistry conversation. Here are a few things I check for.

- How emotionally robust is this client? I am not a therapist and my coachee needs to be fit and well to get the most out of this work.
- How ready are they?
- Have they reached the end of their tether or are they chomping at the bit to do more? These are the clients whose progress I know I can accelerate.
- What's their learning style, energy and language, and how much of a match are these for my skill set and approach?

If I feel that one of the above isn't quite a match I will either recommend checking back in at a later date or offer my feedback on why I think it would be best to consider an alternative approach or coach. If I feel that the person needs more support than I could give, I will let them know. Coaching is an investment of time and money – I don't want to take this money unless I feel quite confident that, together, we can get them where they want to be and enjoy the process too.

At the start line

It's really important to start well. First impressions count and you want to build a strong and firm foundation for your work together. Things to consider are your personal brand, how you show up and how you communicate. Your professionalism matters, and is demonstrated not just by your work but by how easy it is to do business with you and how you present your process. It's the small things such as how easy it is to schedule an appointment, and how you communicate your terms and get contracts signed, that can have you dent the relationship in the first few points of contact. Make sure your payment processing is transparent, easy to understand and simple to complete.

Getting to know your coachee

Before I begin working with a coachee, I take a deep diagnostic. I've formed a questioning document over several years of practice to cover all the key elements I need us to consider. Giving your coachee some reflection activity in advance helps them to get going with the process before your first session. It also literally enables you to be on 'the same page' when it comes to knowing where they are and what matters most to them. Consider designing your own.

In the first meeting, you will want to contract with the client about their expectations for working together and define what will be achieved at each stage. You may find it useful to discuss boundaries, set out your way of working together and explore how you decide on the timing of the next session. I mostly spend session one checking my understanding of our diagnostic document and clarifying the direction of travel we are moving in. I will usually introduce the Career Equation® in this first session as it provides a strong framework for our work together.

In between the sessions

I recommend creating a short, automated review form. This checks in with the coachee 24 hours before your next session and asks them how they got on with any actions set, how they are feeling and what they want to focus on. This is important, because I may have an agenda and a schedule, but it may not be in line with what is currently the coachee's priority. Perhaps a job opportunity has come up suddenly, or there is a crisis at work that is diverting their attention.

These are their sessions and they can use them in whatever way will best serve them to be successful. A heads-up can be useful so you can adjust your plan accordingly.

Who is the client?

Sometimes the person who pays the bill and the person who you work with are different people. You may be contracted by a firm to work with their internal talent on their career navigation. Remember to agree what the outcomes will be between the three of you. Is the agenda for working together clear and transparent – is it to grow them, to support them or to manage them out? To what extent is what the coachee shares confidential? What are the reporting mechanisms and success criteria between the client paying the bill and the client receiving the coaching?

Always agree these up front and revisit and report at the end of the period.

How to end well

I think it is really important to end your coaching relationship well. All too often, we neglect a strong close, which is a shame. The end of a process gives you the opportunity to reflect on the distance travelled, the successes and the challenges, and to offer feedback and insight about how you experienced the other person and they, you. It's a chance to celebrate their new beginnings and the evolution of your relationship over that time.

A good ending also serves you well from a business perspective. Remember that much of your work will come from recommendations, referrals and references. We've had several corporate projects take off on the back of a job well done with an individual coaching client who referred us into their new organization. Remember also to stay in touch. It's very rewarding to follow where your coachees move to as their career grows and grows in line with their design statement.

And finally ...

There are many benefits to running an independent coaching practice as opposed to being in-house. You get to speak freely, without other agendas encroaching on your work. You can hold your coachee to exactly what they want, with complete impartiality. These can be challenging components of working as part of an internal talent coaching team and are among the reasons that many professionals choose to invest their own resources in coaching.

The start of the 2020s has been challenging and eye-opening, with a global pandemic, economic recession, the highest unemployment on record and widespread recognition of systemic racism in the Western world. Many sectors have been fundamentally disrupted. There will be more to come in my view.

In times like these, competent career conversations become an important public service. There is much to be done. Many folk will be seeking a new direction in their work. The Black Lives Matter campaigns have highlighted the systemic inequality in both education and the workplace that impacts worst on young black men. Good career coaching can help to address systemic inequalities, help women, diverse audiences and the older generation recognise their transferable skills, find fulfilling work that suits them and take their first step into entrepreneurship or self-employment. You're in an exciting and rewarding profession for which the need is growing.

If you want to get accredited with us, you can find out more about the process at www.thecareerequation.com/resources.

11 Case studies from career coaches

Generally speaking, a career coaching client will seek out a coach in one of four circumstances:

- returning to work after a break
- looking for a new way to do what they do
- looking for a new start or next step
- making the most of their current role.

Client 1: The returner

Most often this is a woman returning to the workplace after having children. The coachee could also be someone coming back from a sabbatical to study, undertake caring responsibilities or recover from a bout of ill health. The challenge here is defined by the fact that the person returning is not the same person who left – their life experience will have changed them. Their work with you is about integrating that evolution of self and, if appropriate, shaping it into a new chapter or new set of criteria for defining success.

Jo was a successful book editor for a children's educational publisher before she had her first child. After his arrival, she took maternity leave and began to think about what her next role might look like. Her husband took a new job that had them move from Cambridge to Manchester. The Career Equation® helped her discover that what she wanted was a more creative and fun aspect to her work. She now works for CBeebies in Manchester.

Client 2: The shapeshifter

This kind of client likes what they are already doing – they are in the right field and they enjoy it, they are applying their skills in a productive way, and the environment and culture they function in works relatively well – but the challenge here is one of passion and of impact. Ideally, they want to move within their field, change their specialism, expand their reach, while staying in the same profession – but possibly moving sector.

Paola was a lawyer for the family trust funds. She was very good at her job and well recognised for her rigour and intelligence. She came to work with me because she recognised that a lack of partner movement meant it would be difficult to secure a promotion through the ranks in her current firm. Though she enjoyed the work, she thought this presented an opportunity to explore a new direction in the field of law. Through the Career Equation® process, it became clear that she had a deep interest in international and foreign affairs. As Brexit was currently playing out, it seemed like a good time to consider a shift into this interesting arena. Paola decided to take a masters in her subject area in Zurich and now works as a lawyer at the Foreign and Commonwealth Office.

Client 3: The new start or next step

For whatever reason, your coachee has decided it is time for a new chapter. They may have relocated; family or voluntary commitments may require more of their time. They may be searching for a level of flexibility not possible in their sector, or perhaps have had a values shift about the integrity of the work they do or the clients they serve. They may express valid concerns about their profession becoming obsolete. Any manner of things can trigger a genuine interest in a career change.

The same context applies for those at a very senior level, moving out from a partner role or changing their life circumstances as they get ready to retire and redesign their future plans, perhaps with a view to becoming their own boss.

Rob worked in academic libraries. It was ok work, but not very stimulating. He was a very creative, artistic person, with a lovely manner about him. He told me about how he had worked hard to set up a shiatsu practice but had struggled to find enough clients. This had lowered his confidence about ever escaping the library! While the people there were very nice, he craved a more dynamic and energetic culture. The Career Equation® helped Rob to identify his natural talent for helping and offering a service for customers and colleagues. He is now part of the customer experience team for a software firm. You can hear his story in a video case study at: www.thecareerequation.com/resources.

Gemma had the job of her dreams. She headed up a team marketing make-up launches for a very well-known make-up brand. She travelled the world and enjoyed every minute. After she had her first child, she made a request to work part-time. This was refused as the company felt her role could not be done in anything less than full-time hours. Gemma also wanted to move out of London and closer to home, so she reluctantly parted company with the firm. For a period, she enjoyed using her strengths to work with a smaller cosmetics firm, who were delighted to have her insight and experiences. The Career Equation® helped her discover that the smaller firm with the flexible hours was a much better fit. Even better still was the dream of setting up her own business as a career coach. Four years on and this is now a reality.

You can hear Gemma discuss her experience on the Career Equation® website: www.thecareerequation.com/resources.

Client 4: Making the most of my current role

The career coaching process can be really valuable for those either new to their role or well established in a role that they plan to stay in for a while. Reflecting on their definition of success and using the Career Design Statement to achieve clarity about how this role fits into their long-term aspirations can help improve morale, deliver performance improvement and offer insight on the next development goals or role stretches that might deliver more value to the business and more satisfaction to the individual.

In each of these circumstances the same set of skills and the Equation come into play. In each, the tendency is to jump into finding the new role, but the important bit is to step back to determine what experiences they are looking for and then work out where and how they could get it.

Tales from the field

I think you have heard enough from me. It's time to hear the voices of some accredited Your Career Plan coaches. Each coach in this diverse community brings their own style and expertise, and specialises in a variety of different clients and in different languages. Some of these coaches are working independently and some work in-house. What they have in common is the Career Equation® tools and approach, in which they are all accredited.

Let's hear from some of our Your Career Plan accredited coaches about their experiences using the Career Equation® to empower their clients to make the right career choice for them.

Luciana Vargas, mediator and Your Career Plan accredited coach: what is really missing?

My client is passionate about travelling; she has been to all five continents in the world more than once and travels an average of 15 times per year! She speaks three languages – Italian, Spanish and English – and is currently learning German.

While from Rome originally, she moved to London seeking greater work opportunities. In 2019, after living in London for ten years, she decided it was time to relocate again, this time in pursuit of a better quality of life. She now lives in Fuerteventura, in the Canary Islands, and is deeply happy with her new life by the sea.

Careerwise, my client had been in finance for ten years and for the past five years she has been working in the tourism industry, which is fully aligned with her passion for travelling. In spite of that positive change, she was still seeking career fulfilment and felt ungrateful for not being truly happy with all she had achieved so far. Determined to work on this, my client decided to engage in career coaching.

My client found great insight in analysing her career progression through the lenses of the Career Equation®. She felt pleased to see her journey towards securing financial stability, sharpening and applying her best skills, and the career move from finance to her industry of passion, where she finally managed to enjoy a positive environment.

Understanding, through the Career Equation®, that she has never been able to have the impact that really matters to her was a light-bulb moment. Until then she thought of herself as an ungrateful soul for not feeling truly fulfilled in her career, in spite of what she had already achieved. Now, aware of what was really missing, she feels justified and allowed to have her feelings. More importantly, she feels empowered to take action and improve things.

She is currently working with her direct report on a few tweaks she would like to implement to her daily work routine; this should equip and empower her to make the changes to her current role, so she can have the impact she needs to make to experience a thriving career. She is excited to see how these new measures will impact her own and her customers' experience going forward.

Zoe Schofield, Career Matters consultant and Your Career Plan coach: her words, not mine!

My client had lost her career mojo. She was still doing a great job, but an organizational restructure had caused her to feel unhappy, stressed, isolated and as if she was being set up for failure. There was a role for her to apply for in the new structure but the thought of it left her feeling cold, uninspired and thinking there must be another option. The majority of the work wasn't fulfilling any more. She loved her Mondays and Fridays as they gave her the opportunity to do voluntary work that she loved on trips and adventures with adults in the social care sector at one end of the week and supporting parents in the local neonatal unit at the other. She saw these as the bookends that kept her going and functioning at her 'normal' job during midweek.

Starting with a simple question, 'What does career success look and feel like to you?', was such a great starting point for her. She described an environment where she would feel recognised and valued, she would be able to make a tangible difference to people's lives, she would be proud of what she did, feeling a really strong connection morally and ethically to the work, feeling uplifted and sharing her knowledge and skills in a non-competitive environment.

So, when she then drew out a sketch of her career timeline to share with me the high and lows of her career so far, she knew what the future lines would look like if she stayed where she was. When we looked at the highs through the Career Equation® goggles it was so much easier to see those times when she was learning new skills or getting the chance to use her existing ones, where there were strong links to her passions around supporting, encouraging, helping and advising others and where she felt like her work did actually add value.

One of the biggest 'a-ha!' moments for her was when we talked about the impact the environment has on her ability to thrive in her career. I often use the analogy of soil and how the soil where your feet are planted is crucial to enable you to flourish, and just like any plant in the garden you are unique and require certain key components in that soil. Without them you may just survive, but with them you increase your chances of thriving. This analogy really helped her to see what she needed.

Discovering all the key ingredients to her perfect 'career bake' made it so clear to her that her existing employment was never going to match her unique equation!

Imposter syndrome alert

During the conversations she mentioned that she had the opportunity to go to the Bliss Baby Charter Conference in Leicester, in connection with her voluntary neonatal work. In came the 'but I'm not really qualified to go to that, they'll be loads of professionals and experts there'. Would the charity ask you to go if they didn't feel you could or would represent them well? How do you feel when you are in the neonatal unit surrounded by lots of medical professionals? Does that stop you supporting and listening to the parents? What's the worst that could happen? How often will this opportunity come up? What would you say to a colleague or friend in the same situation? We dived right in to get to the heart of the matter and then we explored the positives of what might happen if she went.

Feeling inspired by the work she had done to gain self-knowledge, and knowing that she just couldn't pass up this opportunity, she went to the event. She enjoyed it immensely and made some valuable connections, one of which was talking to an occupational therapist.

Her Career Design Statement, together with the networking and confidence-boosting conference event, was just the trigger she needed to spark something new and take steps towards her new goal ... to become an occupational therapist specializing in neonatal care. When she had explored the role more, she knew it was what she wanted to pursue.

> *I will use my communication and interpersonal skills in listening with care and empathy and my passion for understanding how I can best help and support individuals and their family to put forward ideas and solutions to make a positive and genuine difference and to be listened to as a trusted and experienced, yet friendly professional.*

She got stuck into her career planning, really starting from the point of visualizing the success and walking backwards from that to work out her plan. She began to research qualification routes, funding options and a few conversations followed about deferring her redundancy option.

I was lucky enough to touch base with her recently and she shared a little update. She finishes in her current role at the end of the month and she will have the summer to enjoy with her children, then her university course in occupational therapy starts in September! To say she is excited would be an understatement!

Her words not mine

It's easy for me to talk about what happened in the sessions from my perspective, but at the end of our sessions together back in the autumn of 2019, here are just a few of the words from her in response to the career coaching experience evaluation.

What I have learned about my career development is:

'That I am not confined to the department that I initially qualified/trained in and that I have many years ahead so taking control now and changing direction is achievable.'

The most useful aspect of the career coaching has been:

'Realizing my career goals and aspirations using the Venn Me process. Learning about the importance of environmental fit (for me!)'

On a scale of 1–10 how likely are you to recommend this Career Coaching and please say why:

'10! Mind-blowingly powerful! Just so so so glad I had the opportunity to access it.'

Aneta Jajkowska, Your Career Plan accredited coach: next steps in career development

My client was looking for guidance, steps, clarity in direction or where she can go in terms of her career.

Starting the career coaching journey

After our first introductory session where we had worked on self-discovery to learn what she recognised about herself in terms of behaviours, situations, perceptions, as well as elements that she has recognised less, my follow-on was to pose the question: 'How do you define success in your career?'

Initially it was not easy to get very specific and the conversation was about her personal growth, how to get better at what she was doing and to keep learning. We discussed interests to see how they play a part, and they surrounded things like technology, travel, sustainability, different cultures.

I could see there was a difficulty in connecting this together for my client and she was not feeling there was a clear path on how this can come together.

It felt like this was the right time to introduce the Career Equation®, to show the different elements that are part of the equation and how identifying them all will give the right structure to define her personal elements of the equation, and as part of that journey a picture would start to form.

I did explain there would be moments of doubt and that the Career Matters approach is designed to work through different stages, with a positive, personal outcome, defining the career statement and a plan that would be relevant for her.

We started the Venn Me process in the session, which helped to provide the starting momentum and allowed me to clarify any initial questions that she might have. We focused on the four elements of the Career Equation® and as homework we agreed for my client to continue building the different elements of her Career Equation® with some additional probing questions to help.

Making progress

When we next checked in after a couple of weeks, my client had come prepared with her list for all four elements of the Career Equation®. While she hadn't had time to gather feedback from others, which can be super helpful when trying to identify your skills, passions, impact and perfect environment, we still had a meaningful session and few interesting discoveries took place.

Her skills was the longest list, and some examples included: analytical thinking; business logic; ability to assess new environment quickly and accurately; ability to translate business world to technical world; finding root causes and brainstorming solutions; ability to explain complex things in an easy way appropriate to the audience; good at connecting with people.

It was a great opportunity to help her connect different skills to each other, to ask questions to understand if there are skills that stem from another skill. I used the analogy of a tree branch and asked her to consider what is that main tree branch stemming from the trunk before it splits into smaller further branches, in order to help identify the core skill. She even came up with the idea to create a mind map (or reverse mind map) to discover the BIG branches for her skills, passions, impact and environment.

I also had the chance to clarify why some of the elements may feel similar (i.e. passions and skills). For example her passion about discovering how things work can show up as analytical thinking – one of her skills.

Both explanations helped to turn the slightly concerned face into a smile!

It definitely created the motivation and momentum for her to take these insights away and begin to bring together the most important elements for her in each area and create her own Career Design Statement. I positioned the career statement as a personal paragraph about meaningful and individual elements of the Career Equation® that will form the foundation for discovering next steps in her career.

We're both looking forward to seeing what further discoveries she makes and how she can then start to make informed choices with clarity and confidence.

Karen Walters, an accredited Your Career Plan coach (independent career coach www.linkedin.com/in/karen-walters-ab5a5388/): the oak tree

For health reasons my client had been forced to take a step back from his career for 12 months. He had been quite senior in the organization, so this had hit him hard. He had returned to work six months prior to our meeting in a less senior position, on the recommendation of his GP and the organization. When we met the client was working full-time, in good health and at a stage where he wanted to kickstart his career but was unsure of the direction he wanted to go in, feeling frustrated and disillusioned.

The Career Equation® was a good tool to start the coaching process and the client was happy to 'give it a go'. We did our contracting for the session and agreed the following outcome:

> I am familiar with the key elements of my career equation and I have a high-level understanding of what is important to me; and for me to be successful

I explained the principles of the equation as follows:

> If we want to thrive in our career and feel inspired, content, fulfilled and successful we need to have all the elements that contribute to that in balance first. The Career Equation® is not a mathematical tool – there is no number crunching involved. It is a holistic view of what we need in place to be the best version of ourselves and succeed in our career. It is dependent on a career that is: a good match for our skill set; something that we are passionate about and provides the opportunity for us to have a real impact. Also, there is another important element that underpins this which is the working environment.

As this concept was new to my client, I applied Erica Sosna's analogy of the environment being the soil and the client being the tree. I presented the client with the visualization that their skills, knowledge, experience, passions, hobbies and personal impact lead from their roots into their main core. If the soil is too rocky the tree will find it hard to get the nutrients it needs to keep it healthy, and its growth will be hindered. If the soil is too sandy, the tree will not be well rooted and could topple over. But if the soil is rich in organic matter and well watered, the tree is free to grow deep roots to anchor itself and it will develop and spread unhindered to be the best version of itself (I was sketching diagrams as I was talking).

This visualization worked well and gave the opportunity to add humour, as the client described what sort of tree he wanted to be ('an oak'). I asked him how this resonated with him. The client stated that he had never thought about the importance of the environment before or the effect your passions can have on your drive and enthusiasm. I witnessed the 'a-ha!' moment in his body language.

I asked him the following questions (and have included a summary of his responses):

If I asked you, off the top of your head, to identify your top three skills and passions, what would you say? 'Excellent data analyst and project manager'; 'Performance driven, always meets target'; and 'Competent leader'. I noticed that these were all skills and asked him where, in his selection, did his passions lie. After a short pause he said: 'I am passionate about learning new things and enjoy research, especially historical research.'

What is it that you would do even if you were not paid for it, simply because it is who you are? I gave a personal example about how I automatically go into coaching mode whenever any of my friends and family have issues or problems to overcome – I simply cannot help myself. His response was that he is a natural teacher and involved in his son's education. This is natural to him and something he could never stop doing.

When we think about impact, what business issue or problem would you say you have the greatest ability to help solve or remove? We eventually got to a point where he recognised that he produced reports that are crucial to the organization's success.

When we think about your impact in the wider world, is there a personal legacy that you want to include? 'Inspirational leader and teacher', which he noted was not even remotely related to what he does at the moment.

I asked the client to review the session's outcome, rate his success in meeting it and state action(s) that he will be taking away to work on. He was amazed at how much he had covered in the 40 minutes and rated the session as 'top notch'. His action was to rate his current role against his key skills, to identify how close a fit it was and what was missing.

My energy substantially increased during the session. I was astounded at how well the tool worked with the client and how natural I felt using it. As this was my first time using the tool I had my crib sheet ready to ensure I didn't forget anything, but I found I didn't need to refer to it until the end and that was only to check I hadn't missed anything. I had witnessed the beginning of a transformational change in my client and it felt wonderful to be a part of it.

Ingrid Van Houdt, learning experience senior manager: making a Venn Me

By this stage in our career coaching journey, my client and I had already explored her career timeline, and I had introduced the Career Equation® and asked her to think about the Venn Me process which would help her to identify her own unique Career Design Statement.

In our previous session, she had really gained a good insight about the environment she wants (or doesn't want) to work in and what helps her or hinders her. It became clear that the ideal environment needs to be informal, with a flexible manager who respects her for the things she is doing and sees the added value she can bring, and colleagues who are supportive to each other and willing to go the extra mile.

With the metaphor about the seed in the flowerpot, I explained the Career Equation® once more, to let it resonate. The seed being herself, the soil being the ideal environment, and the water, sun and nutrition reflecting her skills, motivations and things she wants to be recognised for in order to become a flourishing flower and find fulfilment and success in her career.

With this metaphor in mind, we started to explore the homework regarding the Venn Me process.

Mentioning her key skills was quite easy for her, even when checking if those skills would be relevant if money was not an issue. Planning and organizing is definitely one of her key skills, as well as bringing positive energy. She is always the one trying to get the best out of every situation. Furthermore, she is creative, although this skill is hardly used in her current job. Exploring the key skills made clear that this is what she is missing in her current job and why she doesn't feel fully respected for who she is and what she is capable of.

Thinking about her passions was more difficult for her, while she initially was only thinking about her current job. We found out that balance is very important to her – not only a work–life balance, but balance in general. She started talking about the things she had experienced in her life and that she would really want to do something with this. Asking herself the why behind it, she learned that she wants to mean something to people and that it really matters to her to be able to add value. She felt that she would like to give that to other people too. When she spoke about this, I really felt the energy and passion in her voice and attitude. Because of our conversation she picked up the idea again and wanted to explore this further.

Looking at the impact she would like to have was easier now. She struggled with this exercise during the preparation, but because of the conversation and because I asked her to think about a role model, she noticed that she had her own message to bring, that she wanted to be a role model herself and that she had a clear vision and ambition to bring that message across. She wanted to bring calmness and balance into others' lives – get the best out of other people, help them feel motivated and continue to develop the skills she possesses that empower her to do so.

Having discussed all elements of the Career Equation® I then invited her to start thinking about her Career Design Statement, and I'm looking forward to seeing how that develops for her.

Marcie Shaoul, Director of Rolling Stone Coaching and Your Career Plan accredited coach: trailblazing and being true to me

James was a senior leader in the not-for-profit sector at a well-known think tank. He had lost his drive and ambition and was bored. We did an intensive coaching programme during which our main goal was to help him regain his drive. The tools we used were Erica Sosna's 'Career Timeline', 'Career Equation®' and then the 'Career Design Statement'. Delving into the highs and lows of his career enabled James to see that autonomy was really important to him. He could also see that the times when he was able to be creative, think on his feet and lead collaboratively worked really well for him. James was happiest when he was able to spot a need and then implement a solution to fit that need to enable global growth. Using the Career Equation® to drill down to the skills he wanted to make more of and helping him to get a Career Design Statement both really enabled him to get his mojo back in his current job.

> *I, James, will use my skills in understanding and developing radical, progressive economic policy ideas and putting them into simple frameworks, and my passion for learning to contribute practically to radical political policy debates.*
>
> *An environment that is flexible and positive with other radical people from whom I can learn and with whom I can share work is what works best for me.*

With these tools in his belt, he then quickly realised that the current role wasn't right for him and went on to become a CEO of a not-for-profit and is trailblazing on global financial development as we speak.

Marcel Dreef, Dassault Systèmes: getting direction

The Career Equation® was the starting point of a series of coaching sessions with a client I had also worked with two years ago. In the past few years, my client had contributed to a variety of solution consultancy activities in the field of complex software. He felt a desire to expand his responsibilities but wasn't sure in which direction. He also felt a bit restless in his current role, especially as his main customer project did not always require the type of contribution that gives him energy.

As the client's career timeline was something we had covered before, we started our new series of coaching conversations with the introduction of the Career Equation® and agreed to explore the components of it together as the basis for next steps. I shared my own Career Design Statement as well as Erica's to give an impression of what we were working towards and explained how it has helped me in making smaller and bigger decisions in my professional life.

After the introduction of the equation as well as the Venn Me concept in our first meeting, the client brought to our second meeting input for his Venn Me diagram. For this he tapped, among others, into notes from our earlier coaching conversations and brainstormed with people close to him to get his flow of ideas going.

In our meeting we talked through the four circles, and even through a first version of the Career Design Statement that the client had drafted.

My client found it both fun and challenging to work through the skills, passion, impact and environment circles in Venn Me. For the skills and passion parts he had come up with a good basis, and for environment he could also communicate well what works and doesn't work for him. Coming up with a sharp way of articulating the impact he aims for proved more challenging.

For me, the most valuable part of the process was the opportunity to talk through the client's Venn Me content. It gave me the opportunity to ask questions about the client's previous experiences, learn about concrete examples and how he felt in these situations, and also to just encourage my client and confirm that some parts really matched the impression I had based on our previous interaction. At the same time this detailed walk-through enabled me to come up with suggestions on how to improve other parts and challenge some of the conclusions.

We wrapped up the Venn Me part by the client scoring each of the four aspects of the Career Design Statement against his current role. He knew that his current role didn't give him energy but wasn't able to explain why. The scoring brought a very clear answer: in his current role the client scored high on passion and skills, but very low on impact and environment.

A nice surprise for me came in our third meeting. The initial draft Career Design Statement didn't feel sufficiently sharp, either for me or for my client.

Something was missing, as was also clear from the lack of enthusiasm my client felt when reading it out loud. After talking through his Venn Me and going over the structure of the Career Design Statement again together, the client embraced the iterative process of crafting his own statement and committed to sharpening it for our next meeting. Instead of just bringing an updated statement, however, he explained with a smile how he had already woven it into his LinkedIn profile summary as it just felt like a natural thing to do after gaining this clarity.

It was rewarding to hear the energy in the voice of the client when he read his final Career Design Statement:

> *I will use my skills in ramping up fast on new domains, structuring complex scenarios and presenting quality visual deliverables, and my passion for learning and working on multidisciplinary domains with technology and people, to deliver tangible and meaningful work that helps improve efficiency and people.*
>
> *An environment that is dynamic and intellectually challenging, where sustainability and people matter and help me improve and expand my horizon, works best for me.*

Structuring the experience of the client in the four categories of the Career Equation® made it relatively easy to identify the gaps between his desired contribution and his current role, and to focus our conversation on the areas where he would like to make adjustments.

Discussing and writing down his thoughts about passion, skills, and in particular impact and environment, also proved to be a good basis for my client a few weeks later for articulating his preferred professional focus in the mid-year review with his manager.

With the clarity the Career Design Statement had provided him, my client realised that the years before had been about exploring options and experiencing a variety of tasks and project contributions, while it is now time to 'start moving towards the centre of his Venn Me diagram'. While my client carefully prepared a pitch for his manager about formalizing and expanding a contribution to a company-wide initiative in the field of sustainability, he was positively surprised when his manager responded with a clear 'yes' and asking what my client would need from him to make it happen.

My client concluded that he might have been negotiating with himself, making assumptions about how others would feel about his desire to tweak his professional focus. He was limiting his own possibilities. With the clarity of the Career Design Statement under his belt, and some renewed energy from the insights the process brought him, he is now ready for starting the next chapter in his professional journey. As my client put it: 'I was well positioned, I had all the skills I needed, so it was mostly a matter of taking two steps back and saying – wait a minute, where do I want to go? That's what the Career Design Statement gave me – direction.'

12 How the Career Equation® works for organizations

Most of this book has been dedicated to the use of the Career Equation® to support individuals to have more clarity and direction in in their work life aspirations through 121 conversations. I believe that the opportunity to be heard, acknowledged and seen for who you are and what you long for remains one of the most powerful gifts we can give to another human being. The more we practise this kind of seeing, the better we are able to acknowledge and enjoy the rich diversity of talents and backgrounds that make up the human experience.

While my day-to-day work includes a number of these conversations, the majority of the consulting my company Erica Sosna's Career Matters undertakes is to deliver this empowering experience on a group level, rather than one-to-one. These programmes have the benefit of both scale and reach, enabling many people in the business to benefit from the insight they provide and helping the Career Equation® and the tools associated with it to 'go viral' in the business and become embedded as standard language and practice.

With this in mind, I've set out a few stories about how this model and method can reach and empower large numbers of people in your company, and offered some tips and tools for ensuring that the company gets as much benefit as possible from using the Career Equation® in their daily work.

Case Study 1: The Open University

The Open University has always been a huge pioneer of accessible, remote learning. When remote learning and digital education were still unimaginable at most mainstream universities, the institution dedicated itself to reaching non-traditional students where they were – out in the community, in care and prison systems, and offering them the opportunity to learn and grow. With 50 years under its belt, the university wanted to support its staff to be as agile as possible in the management of their careers. The world has changed and now many universities and HE colleges offer learning at a distance. To move forward, survive and thrive, everyone in the talent pool needed to play their part.

Unlike many organizations that work with us, The Open University had excellent tenure and did not suffer a brain drain. The culture and values of the organization were appealing and inspiring and it was considered a nice place to work where there were good opportunities to keep exploring and try something new. However, many of the administrative and academic staff at the university felt that their ability to make best use of these opportunities through internal mobility was slowed down by a combination of a lack of clarity about what they wanted, lowered confidence about their ability to be successful in the application process and challenges in navigating the process itself, which was rigorous and demanding.

Our first pilots provided groups of self-nominated individuals from across the university the chance to explore what the Career Equation® could give them. We combined our end-to-end career design approach with key insights on the changing world of work and on how the new trends in workplace design and aspiration provided both crisis and opportunity. The day finished with practical education in how to articulate and demonstrate transferable skills.

It was fantastic to see how eye-opening this macro-perspective was. In addition, we were pleased with how quickly the staff accelerated their ability to imagine what could be next for them, using just a little applied focus and the model of the Career Equation®. In the light of the pilots, we decided to design and run two short follow-on sessions. These were designed to support employees through the application process for new roles, providing an opportunity to practise conveying their value and aspirations in both the written format of a role application or CV and the spoken word, by putting their best foot forward at interview.

As the programme rolled out over 24 months, we started to receive a number of personal emails from participants. They wanted to write to us to share their success in applying for and securing roles at a range of levels across the organization. This was particularly gratifying, because like many academic institutions, The Open University had a very structured set of hierarchical levels through which one would normally progress step by step. What became clear was that, having now crystallised what they were looking for and what they could offer, several of the participants were 'leapfrogging' the traditional level structure and were able to position themselves as worthy candidates for roles way beyond where they would have felt they had 'permission' to aim.

While many of these successes related to taking on more senior roles, for some their internal mobility related more to the opportunity to try something new. Having perhaps felt a little pigeonholed by a reputation for excellence in a key narrow field, the Career Equation® was empowering them to reposition or rebrand themselves in a way that enabled hiring managers to put their trust in them and take a calculated risk to secure the right person for the right role.

Either way, these moves constructively challenged some of the cultural norms that were unwittingly slowing down the progress of talent. By going for what they wanted and succeeding, these participants showed the university that future potential and commitment to a new direction, rather than just previous experience, could be a valid way to measure ability and role fit. Overall, there have been huge strides made in talent mobility, and the ability of the university to make best use of their loyal and committed population has increased exponentially.

In total 376 people took the programme over the 24-month period. We continue to work with the university to deliver the programme virtually, enabling those in the Hub regions beyond the Milton Keynes headquarters to benefit from the tools in the Career Equation® toolbox.

Case Study 2: High potentials in a world-class financial institution

Competition for the very best people remains high in the financial services sector. Our client was an entrepreneurial new entity that has 'spun out' of a world-class group of financial services organizations. Their Head of Talent had developed a global development programme for their top talent, those first in line to succeed the C-Suite of this 30,000-strong company. With an inspiring new CEO at the helm, who has a deep commitment to development and education, she had a strong mandate to take action and pilot a programme that would deliver real results for this population.

In the first year we worked with this client, we had identified that there was a genuine gap around career clarity. Although these were the most talented and ambitious amongst their population, they still struggled to articulate a concrete set of aspirations for themselves. This proved tricky when it came to helping them make the right decisions in their strategic moves within the business. This was not helped by the fact that a huge review of the company's core offers was underway and the strategic plan was being revitalised, generating a lot of uncertainty, which is rarely a good climate for talent stability. In addition, this division of the group was characterised by a more agile and entrepreneurial spirit and culture than the wider divisions, making a speedy response vital to meet the needs of this rapidly growing firm.

To keep the very best people, we knew that the more insight the Head of Talent had about their 'direction of travel', the more able she and the senior team would be to customise the employee experience and exposure to the right growth opportunities for this community. The more tailored that experience became, the more invested they felt and the less likely we were to lose them.

In Year 1, the career planning aspect of the programme, together with the Career Equation®, was delivered as part of an in-person two-day final module near HQ. By this point in the eighteen-month development journey, attrition of this population had been high. We realised that, to maximise engagement and benefit, we needed to feature the career clarity process much earlier in the development journey.

In Year 2, we introduced the Career Equation® work within the first six months of programme. In addition, we built up a blended learning approach, reducing the need for travel. The digital aspects of the programme were delivered via video and email, while the live virtual sessions were conducted in small coaching groups online. This gave the participants the chance to reflect over an extended period, rather than just in a one-day in-person session, and also gave space for each person to discuss their hopes and desires in a group of six, thus building a strong sense of intimacy and community. Another innovation for this year was the active involvement of managers. We developed a series of videos to empower managers to feel confident to respond to the outputs of the Career Equation® process and structure a quality conversation about the future with their team members.

Lastly, the Head of Talent received Career Design Statements from each of her talent population and followed up with one-to-one conversations with each of them to help further shape their career plans and support them in their goals. Within the period of the eighteen-month journey, 30 per cent of the participants secured a more senior role and all of them left with a much more specific and nuanced definition of what success meant to them and the actions they would take to evolve themselves for the next chapter in their career journey. Retention in Year 2 was also massively improved. Just one person left the firm to return to their previous profession, having discovered from their Career Equation® process that that was the ideal work for them! The company were sad to lose him but delighted that the process led to a deep level of career clarity for him. It also felt the right thing to do for their employer brand as he would certainly share the investment the company made in him in helping him identify the right definition of career success for him.

We look forward to continuing to evolve this process in Year 3. Our ultimate aim will be to embed the entire process internally, with the Head of Talent and the managers taking on the driving forward of career conversations and capturing these in a meaningful way.

Case Study 3: An organization-wide approach from Dassault Systèmes

Dassault Systèmes focuses its business on imagining virtual worlds. Whether under the ground, in the sky, on land or sea, it imagines and envisions possibilities using its cutting-edge technology. Dassault Systèmes has grown inorganically, through strategic acquisitions and is headquartered in Paris.

This acquisition strategy has meant that it can feel a little complicated to navigate the range of opportunities that exist in the business. There are a large range of different brands under various umbrellas relating to healthcare, geology, aeronautics and buildings, to name just a few key segments. In this context, it can be overwhelming to have so many interesting choices. In addition, the business is very dynamic and disruptive, frequently reinventing its core teams to stay ahead of trends and changing customer needs. So, nothing stays the same for long! Lastly, as an innovation-led business, employees can show initiative and create their own roles in response to a business opportunity. It is a vivid environment in which to work and explore. Dassault Systèmes hires very bright, technically skilled talent. This is a population that accumulates a huge amount of expertise over time and is very valuable to retain.

Dassault Systèmes is very committed to the development and advancement of its people. To this end, alongside its corporate 'university', which provides role-specific executive education, it has designed a number of its own career management tools. '*My Journey*' provides a career route map based on previous roles that talent has had in the business. It gives employees the opportunity to capture their current work projects, career aspirations and key skills and helps them to create a shortlist of roles that match them. However, take-up hasn't been as the company would hope and the sense is that the array of opportunities and directions in the business could be leading to individuals finding themselves in roles that are not the perfect fit, when that perfect fit could well exist in the company.

We've been able to work with the EMEA (Europe and Middle East) to trial a number of interesting career programmes with a range of different audiences. This has helped different populations across the business embrace the Career Equation® as their go-to model for conducting career conversations and navigating their internal moves within the business to make the most of these opportunities. These programmes have included international webinars for employees and quick virtual classes for managers on the key components of an effective career conversation. We've helped the mentoring population, both mentor and mentee, get into career conversation mode and new graduates to feel better equipped to make specialist selections at the end of their rotations. Lastly, we now work with the in-house HR population and a wider coaching community, to equip them to use the Your Career Plan coaching method for 121 conversations with their talent.

As a result, we are starting to see a real uptick in mobility and career clarity amongst many levels of talent. As understanding of the importance of career conversations grows, senior leaders have become more open about sharing their stories of their career history, decision making and the different areas of the business and what they offer. Our next project will be to align the '*My Journey*' app with the appropriate structures and skills of quality career coaching conversations to encourage user take-up. I believe that this app, with its 'skills passport' structure, could be a powerful way to support internal development and mobility alongside an explicit and exciting career plan for each employee. When your people can see a future in your business and know that it includes them in the road map, you are always much more likely to retain them.

Case Study 4: International property company bespoke programme

Our relationship with the company began with an introduction to the Head of Learning and Development. An innovator, people person and expert coach, they have been part of the company's DNA for more time than they care to remember! In their role, they have helped the property business to evolve its managerial and leadership education for over 30,000 staff worldwide.

The company is a world-class place to learn about estate management, surveying, planning, development, and commercial and residential deal making.

What I most appreciate about the Head of Learning and Development has been their openness to discovery. Their first question to me was 'Why would we want to discuss careers with our people?' To their credit, they took on board my responses and became interested in how the material could be embedded into an even better experience for talent in the business. The company, unlike many of our other clients, does not have a retention 'issue'. People love working there and have long tenure in the company. But this creates its own challenges as opportunities to progress can become limited when everyone loves their work so much that they stay where they are!

We began by dipping our toe in the water of the manager development programme, to sense how the Career Equation® might land with a high-potential population. When this went well, we moved on to equipping the Head of Learning and Development with the Your Career Plan method and tools. As their knowledge deepened, it started to become clear that there were a range of ways in which this work could be useful to supporting the population in the business. One of the most interesting and exciting of these was the opportunity to work with directors with a long tenure in the business. Valued experts, it was critical that this population had something of a plan for their next decade in the sector and that succession planning could be undertaken to ensure the expert knowledge they had acquired, of clients, contracts and how to make things happen in their field, was not lost as they moved towards the later stages of their careers.

The UK managing director was absolutely committed to making sure they are well supported to explore the moves that felt most interesting to them and that they have the opportunity to reflect on their career so far and make some conscious goals and plans, not just for their continued career in the business, but also their life beyond it.

This year we will pilot a bespoke programme just for them. The intention of this programme is to empower the company's talent, later in their careers, to make plans that excite and energise them for sharing their expertise, extending client reach, building out their next career moves and taking care of their personal goals, health and relationships. We're very excited to see how the Career Equation® could help this population formulate a refreshing set of career plans that power them into an exciting future.

Case Study 5: Championing the cause

Whether it is getting more women into senior roles, addressing systemic racism and inequality, or supporting those returning to the workplace after a period of ill health, we are often invited to bring the Career Equation® into the room. The model offers a fantastic framework for helping all levels of talent across all industries to define and clarify the experiences they are looking for in the world of work. A lack of clarity causes inaction. Over and over again, we have found that once people really know what they want and are supported with the tools to turn those aspirations into action, they are empowered for a lifetime. It is a particular pleasure for me to bring this work to those who deserve it most. Those who have not been born into privilege or gone to the best schools. For me, the class barriers of the elite in the UK are taking our economy into a nose-dive. They don't represent or capture the vibrancy and ability of the diverse country that I am proud to call my home. The Career Equation® can quickly level the playing field and we are always interested to do work that moves this needle.

If you think we can help and you are inspired by these case studies, do drop me a line.

13 Some final thoughts on the future of work

What does the future hold for careers? The Covid-19 pandemic has certainly accelerated some of the key trends I envisaged some years ago. At last, the possibility of delivering high-quality, senior work at a distance, working flexibly, has been proved workable in many industries. Of course, there are some in which we would very much want in-person contact with a real person, and that will never go away. Yet the pandemic opened up awareness of a global market for talent and the possibility that a virtual team could deliver to a high standard beyond the workspace. We met a few cats and children, we learned more about one another and, in doing so, also widened the perspective of what elements of ourselves we might bring to work. I think the reduced formality of these times and the greater intimacy imposed by a mortal challenge did us some good and perhaps took us a little further in both humanizing the workplace and, on an individual basis, thinking more deeply about the link between work and personal satisfaction.

I maintain my prediction that the hours we work and the place it holds in our lives will shift for many during my time on earth and that of the next generation. Back in the days before the Industrial Revolution, many worked just the amount needed to keep life steady. Work also took place more in family groups. This reluctance to over-exert oneself in the UK led to a fictional Saint, Saint Monday, being created to justify a four-day week. I hope we might see his Saint's day become a national institution, and see everyone working fewer hours than they have in the last couple of decades.

For companies, the locations we work in, the work we do, who does it and when it is done will continue to evolve. This will mean less simple job titles and more flexible and fluid definitions of who does what. How this will be formalised, recognised and rewarded will be of interest, as well as changes in the number of contracts offered on a permanent and full-time basis.

We have seen, from the Millennial generation onwards, a reluctance to compromise on the need for work to matter. I think this aspiration for purpose and meaning in our work will continue to grow, as long as the economic and social circumstances allow it to do so. The more, then, that we commit to talking about what matters to each person and really listening to the answers, the better able we will be to fine-tune both the work at hand and our people strategies to create a win/win for employer and employee alike.

As we enter a new climate in which we are expected to work until later in life, it is my hope that the opportunity for reinvention will inspire experienced talents and older generations to take on study, work and mentoring that moves them. Our current pilot work focuses on meeting the needs of the later stage of the professional career and I am excited to see where this takes us and our participants.

Workplaces have their own work-to-do bias, institutional levels of bias and systemic discrimination. To me, this work goes hand in hand with the environmental piece of the Career Equation®. Part of the power of this work is that it gives a voice to what needs to shift in a culture in order for everyone to thrive and to progress based on merit, not the colour of their skin, the gender they identify with or who they know.

My deep hope, and probably the next chapter of my own career, is that we forge stronger connections between the education environment and the world of employment. There is a need for much greater alignment and relevance between the school curriculum and workplace skills and activities. The curriculum has long needed an overhaul, but until education is divorced from politics, it will be challenging to develop a lasting long-term shift in emphasis. In the meantime, I hope that by introducing Career Equation® models and tools to younger people and their educators, we will be able to ensure that our future generations choose rather than fall into their careers, and do this on the basis of a rewarding and confidence-building level of self-knowledge. Then they will know where to put their own 6-year-old passion, whether it is for magic, science, people or song, and find it welcomed in the workplace.

Thank you to my team at Career Matters. Oana, Zoe, Jane you are the corners to my square. To our clients, who trusted us with a whole new agenda in their companies and workplaces and who generously gave their time and perspective to this book. Special thanks to Ruth Barnes, Aneta Jajkowska and Krissie Haigh, who have been way more than clients and more like 'champions' of the sisterhood. Thanks also to Laura at McGraw-Hill for approaching me with enthusiasm and really believing in this book, and to my first reader Denise McQuaid who gave me confidence to continue. Most of all, thanks to my husband Peter and my little son Barney, who adventured through bursts of time without me during the intense UK lockdown of 2020 to allow me to birth this literary babe. And thanks to my readers, coachees, peers and friends, who have taken on the input from the Career Equation® and used it to enhance their experience of the mysterious and magical experience that is this thing we call life.

Index

Page numbers in italics are figures.